Volume 17, Number 4   **2002**

Contents

Subscriber Information

Journal of Mass Media Ethics (ISSN 0890–0523) is published quarterly by Lawrence Erlbaum Associates, Inc., 10 Industrial Avenue, Mahwah, NJ 07430–2262. Subscriptions for the 2002 volume are available only on a calendar-year basis.

Printed journal subscription rates are $35.00 for individuals and $320.00 for institutions within the United States and Canada; $65.00 for individuals and $350.00 for institutions outside the United States and Canada. Order printed subscriptions through the Journal Subscription Department, Lawrence Erlbaum Associates, Inc., 10 Industrial Avenue, Mahwah, NJ 07430–2262.

Electronic: Full price print subscribers to Volume 17, 2002 are entitled to receive the electronic version free of charge. Electronic-only subscriptions are also available at a reduced price of $288.00 for institutions and $31.50 for individuals.

Change of Address: Send change-of-address notice to Journal Subscription Department, Lawrence Erlbaum Associates, Inc., 10 Industrial Avenue, Mahwah, NJ 07430–2262.

Claims for missing issues cannot be honored beyond 4 months after mailing date. Duplicate copies cannot be sent to replace issues not delivered due to failure to notify publisher of change of address.

Journal of Mass Media Ethics is abstracted or indexed in *Communication Abstracts; Communication Institute for Online Scholarships; Columbia Journalism Review; ComIndex; Media and Values; Nordicom Finland; Public Affairs Information Service; Com Abstracts; Humanities Index; Humanities Abstracts;* EBSCO*host* Products.

Microform copies of this journal are available through ProQuest Information and Learning, P.O. Box 1346, Ann Arbor, MI 48106–1346. For more information, call 1–800–521–0600, ext. 2888.

Requests for permission should be sent to the Permissions Department, Lawrence Erlbaum Associates, Inc., 10 Industrial Avenue, Mahwah, NJ 07430–2262.

Journal of Mass Media Ethics, *17*(4), 261–262
Copyright © 2002, Lawrence Erlbaum Associates, Inc.

Foreword

In early November 2001, less than 2 months after the September 11 tragedies in New York, Washington, and Pennsylvania abruptly thrust Americans and the world into a new sense of global vulnerability, a group of scholars gathered at Washington and Lee University to advance ideas on whether there can be a universal set of moral values toward which media professionals may look for guidance. It was the second annual colloquium and conference on Mass Media and Applied Ethics, organized under the difficult post 9/11 circumstances by Lou Hodges.

The task, of course, was a product of the ever-hopeful view that a world composed of human beings (with all the commonalities that suggests) can surely unite on values as important as the means by which they receive information, and the types of information contained in those sources.

The search and its products, as they unfolded over several days, appeared, at once, to range from hopeful to futile, but never definitive. An effective global code may well be written and buried deep in someone's files, but the scholars gathered in Virginia, and their papers demonstrated it certainly hasn't risen on the radar to universal practical acceptance. Not even a half-century of the United Nation's Declaration on Human Rights have achieved that goal in more than an abstract, lip-service way. Indeed, those conference scholars whose works appear in this special issue of the *Journal of Mass Media Ethics* both challenge and reinforce conventional wisdom; at least one candidly suggests topics to be considered in drafting such a code, but none declared their confidence that a code was forthcoming.

Given the sharp global divisions, even the division between liberal and traditional cultures, it will take an almost miraculous transformation in attitudes at all levels before a universal code, even one merely explicating ideals, will become a fact of media life. Yet, the search has been a useful and enlightening one, as the articles in this issue attest.

An entertaining and useful centerpiece launches the discussion here by noting that the global standby virtue of truth should be a first casualty of the universal quest. Herb Strentz of Drake University suggests four standards that tend to be universal, but need discussion to attach themselves to journalism. Such standards are as follows: use restraint, know thyself, respect others, and be accountable. He points out that a great deal of ethics lies in the moment-to-moment decisions of journalists, undergirded by some commitment to principle. Hence, his standards, or principles. Ethical standards are, he argues, goals and not habits. His significant omission, of course, is truth telling, though he recognizes the importance of truth and devotes considerable space to justifying its absence from his list.

From Spain, Roberto Herrscher looks at the ambiguity of codes relative to those who use them. That is, the same words mean different things and call for different defense when journalists, media owners, or audience members cite their expectations. He leads his principles list with adherence to truth, although he recognizes many of the problems Stentz identified. Other principles are completeness, conflict of interest, freedom–independence–self-esteem, honesty, respect for privacy, treatment of powerless groups, and importance and relevance. He does not propose a solution, but does explore some principles and complexities that attend to universal applications in the media environment: culture, politics, and free enterprise.

In a more abstract approach, Dennis Cali of East Carolina university sees the September 11, 2001, attacks on New York and Washington creating the need for a commitment to global communitarianism to align powerful western media (plagued by individualism) and the rest of the world (with a cultural communitarian bent).

American University's Rick Rockwell notes practical problems, especially for management, as he examines the aftermath of a code drafting program for Central American journalists (conducted at Florida International University), declaring that long-term effects have been minimal. Editors who participated in the program noted they never read the New Orleans declaration, and several examples suggest the Declaration may have been more window dressing than source of substantive guidance for media executives.

An excerpt from the keynote speaker concludes the conference texts in this issue. Kevin Klose of National Public Radio cited the relation between listener and radio, posing the choice for the listener (assuming effective radio news) as one between ignorance and freedom.

Publication by alternative newspaper *Boston Phoenix* of photos of the Daniel Pearl slaughter (with a link to a gory video Web site) occupy commentators in Cases and Commentaries, and the Book Review section examines four recent books and lists several books relevant to media ethics recently received by the Book Review editor.

A very successful Colloquium Three, on cyber use and media ethics, was held at the University of Illinois in October 2002, with Cliff Christians at the helm, and the fourth will be at University of South Florida–St. Petersburg, March 18–19, 2003. Jay Black is the organizer. The colloquia are jointly sponsored by hosting institutions: the *Journal of Mass Media Ethics*, the Brigham Young University Department of Communications, and Lawrence Erlbaum Associates, Publishers.

The Editors

Journal of Mass Media Ethics, 17(4), 263–276
Copyright © 2002, Lawrence Erlbaum Associates, Inc.

Universal Ethical Standards?

Herb Strentz
Drake University

❏ *If a quest for universal ethical standards in journalism is to be productive, we should first be able to articulate an overarching set of universal ethical standards that can apply across cultures, across ethical schools of thought, across professions. In this article I offer 4 likely universal standards that have relevance to journalism, suggesting universal journalism standards can also be identified. Although these and other standards will not be panaceas for the ethical dilemmas journalists often face, they provide needed anchors for decision making.*

If we are to undertake "a renewed quest for universal ethical standards in *journalism*," we should be able to articulate at least a few universal standards to assure ourselves that the journalism quest has potential. We also should illustrate that the broader standards are applicable to journalism.

Otherwise, why begin the journalism quest?

Logically, universal ethics should satisfy, or at least not be inconsistent with, the core principles of the major ethical schools of thought—including teleological or utilitarian approaches, the deontological or duty-driven approach of Immanuel Kant, Aristotle's Golden Mean, Judeo-Christian tenets, and so forth. Although this article may suffer from a Western orientation, the universal nature of values it offers is not contradicted by discussions of Hindu, Buddhist, Confucian, Islamic, and other non-Western cultures reviewed in the course of developing the article (Christians & Traber, 1997; Merrill, 1994; Saunders, 1934; Wiener, 1974).

In this article I seek to identify a handful of possible universal values and briefly discuss how these values are applicable to the practice of journalism.

Been There, Done That?

John Merrill (1989) reviewed the quest for wide-ranging journalistic ethics in the context of concerns of the 1970s and 1980s with regard to the New World Information Order and controversies over the relationship between government and the press.

Merrill (1989) wrote that Nordenstreng, then-president of the International Organization of Journalists,

> has asserted that an international journalistic ethics "implies two significant steps beyond what is typically held in the libertarian tradition with its passion to remain free from any socio-political obligations other than the pursuit of truth": (1) an invitation for the journalist to support a number of universally recognized ideals and to fight corresponding evils, and (2) an awareness that universal values are vital constituents of the profession of journalism—such values being a commitment to truth, integrity, and other characteristics of professionalism. (p. 217)

Along those lines, after meetings in Paris and Prague in 1983, the Fourth Consultative Meeting of the International and Regional Organizations of Working Journalists[1] advanced 10 ethical principles to guide and inspire journalistic codes of ethics.

These principles, briefly stated, called for the following:

1. Rights to acquire accurate information and rights to free expression.
2. Unbiased, in-depth reporting.
3. Accountability to the public.
4. High standards of journalistic integrity.
5. Access to information.
6. Protection of privacy.
7. Respect for community and democratic values.
8. Respect for universal values and cultural diversity.
9. Commitment to the elimination of war and other social evils, such as racism, colonialism, and poverty.
10. Promotion of a New World Information Order that would restructure the international communications system (Merrill, 1989, pp. 219–220).

In 1980, the United Nations Educational, Scientific, and Cultural Organization (UNESCO) International Commission for the Study of Communication Problems published its report (*Many Voices*, 1980) that discussed norms of professional conduct for journalists and reported that

> there is general recognition of the fact that journalists have responsibilities not only vis-à-vis their own convictions but also towards the public. Summarily, four kinds of responsibilities may be defined: (a) contractual responsibility in relation to the media and their internal organization; (b) social responsibility entailing obligations towards public opinion and society as a whole; (c) responsibility or liability deriving from the obligation to comply with the law; (d) responsibility towards the international community, relat-

ing to respect for universal values. These four types of responsibility may in certain respects be contradictory or even conflicting. (p. 241)

The range of concerns and issues addressed by Nordenstreng, the MacBride Commission, and others was as daunting as it was provocative—provocative but not altogether productive. The global ethics discussion became entangled in issues related to the New World Information Order and, eventually, the United States' withdrawal from UNESCO. International codes also may founder because of ambition and specificity. They try to do too much—end wars, protect privacy, and make sure journalists spelled names correctly!

> *International codes ... try*
> *to do too much.*

Perhaps a more helpful approach is found in the work of Christians and Traber (1997) as they surveyed cultures around the world to identify universal values, or "ethical protonorms." Traber concluded that

> certain ethical protonorms—above all, truth-telling, commitment to justice, freedom in solidarity [freedom blossoming in an attitude of responsibility for each other], and respect for human dignity—are validated as core values in communications in different cultures. These values are called universal not just because they hold true cross-culturally. ... The universality of these values ... is rooted ontologically in the nature of human beings. It is by virtue of what it means to be human that these values are universal. (p. 341)

Cued by Christians and Traber (1997) this article starts with ethical concerns in general and moves to journalism. That path seems less tortuous than focusing on journalism alone and being overwhelmed by the burdens and challenges journalists face in a global context.

Three Ground Rules

At the outset it should be recognized that, by definition, "universal standards" will be general in nature, perhaps disappointingly so. Just as they will not solve global problems they will not provide ready solutions or be panaceas for many nitty-gritty issues in journalism—such as under what circumstances it is ethical to identify a crime victim. On the other hand, the articulation of even general ethical standards should suggest that some of the routine arguments against such efforts need not discourage us from our journalism quest.

For example, at the outset, we should dispense with the notion that widespread or long-term acceptance of a practice by a particular culture or society is sufficient evidence that the practice is ethical, relatively speaking of course. Racism, genocide, and other evils have been widely practiced and well established in one society or another; however, no one defends such practices as ethical. Further, we should be able to demonstrate that every situation is not necessarily or routinely different, that our universal standards—as simple as they might be—are not situational. Such a view runs counter to the it-all-depends answer frequently given when journalists are asked about news coverage ethics. Such a response is invoked so often that one can imagine a journalist offering this response when a spouse asks, "What time will you be home from work, dear?"

Well, it all depends. Maybe I'll run off with a news source and never see you and the children again. Maybe I'll get upset at the office and assault Henry and have to spend the night in jail. Maybe I'll get picked up for shoplifting that toy we so desperately want for Junior but cannot afford. You just never know.

But you *should* know. In most contexts and relationships, people should (and do) know what to expect of one another.

Universal standards—even if identified and agreed on—would not be cost free. The notion that an ethical act is one that does not harm or injure someone, as compassionate and desirable as that may be, cannot withstand even cursory analysis. After all, what makes many ethical decisions so vexing—why they are dilemmas—is that someone may suffer as a result of an ethical act. That condition is worsened for the conscientious journalist because, although one may escape immediate harm from an ethical act, others may suffer.[2]

Rationally, we should be willing to accept the consequences of our actions. If we do something wrong, we may figure we deserve whatever punishment is in store for us; we knew the risks going in, so we shouldn't complain about consequences. A journalist's contract often is not that simple. The journalist may do right in reporting details of a death, divorce, crime, bankruptcy, and so on. However, it is not the journalist who suffers from such publicity. The journalist can understand why it is important to report the address of a home that was burglarized and can recite the ethical argument for doing so. But the 85-year-old widow who lives in the home may be fearful of the burglar's return. If so, she will view a news report as invasive and will not be assuaged by the journalist's argument that her fears are unwarranted or, if warranted, part of the price that must be paid in an open society.

One final thought on being cost free: Perhaps this, or any, search for ethical standards is confounded by the thought, or desperate hope, that recognition and acceptance of such standards will make life easier for all concerned, saving both time and anguish. Knowing the right thing to do, however, does not make a decision easier or less grievous. For example, even if one's parent has signed a living will, stipulating that no heroic measures be taken to prolong life, that provision does not lessen the trauma or the grief of the survivors' decision to "pull the plug." All a living will provides is confidence that perhaps the decision is the right one. Maybe that is the most we can ask.

---

*Knowing the right thing to do
does not make a decision easier.*

This article's understanding of ethics follows that of Isaiah Berlin (1980):

Ethical thought consists of the systematic examination of the relations of human beings to each other, the conceptions, interests, and ideals from which human ways of treating one another spring, and the systems of value on which such ends of life are based. These beliefs about how life should be lived, what men and women should be and do, are objects of moral inquiry; and when applied to groups and nations, and, indeed, mankind as a whole, are called political philosophy, which is but ethics applied to society. (pp. 1–2)

Consequently, we approach ethics in the context of community. In the profound insight of Merrill (1989, who may have been paraphrasing Sartre), "we are individuals who create ourselves as we interact with others."

Four Standards

With an ethic of reciprocity in mind, this article advances four universal standards as starting points. At best, these standards suggest it is not folly to proceed in a quest for universal ethical standards in journalism. The remainder of the article lists and discusses the standards in a journalistic context.

Use Restraint: Violence should never be the first resort in conflict resolution.
Know thyself: Self-deception—lying to oneself—is not a healthy practice for an individual or for a society.
Respect others: Do not abuse one's authority or stewardship.
Be accountable: One bears responsibility for the consequences of one's actions.

Applications to Journalism: Starting Points

If the previous four general standards are universal, they should be applicable to journalism. To that end, here are a few of the conditions that help shape the discussion about applications to journalism (with apologies for what may be obvious):

Journalism with a news orientation rules out government information programs—setting aside much of the controversy involving what was called the New World Information Order. The following discussion tries to apply the ethical standards without emphasis on First Amendment protection, necessary if standards are to be global.

Nonetheless, the power and popularity of the idea of free expression is undeniable. Although the First Amendment is not exportable, Article 19 of the United Nations Declaration of Human Rights states, "Everyone has the right to freedom of opinion and expression; this right includes freedom to hold opinions without interference and to seek, receive and impart information and ideas through any media and regardless of frontiers" (p. 19). Granted, the history of the Declaration and Article 19 is United States influenced. Further, widespread adherence to Article 19 and whether it would be adopted today are open to question. Nevertheless, Article 19 remains on the books, and a universal standard of journalism ethics would ignore that only at its peril (*Many Voices*, 1980).

Given constraints of space, this discussion does not explore existing codes, such as those of the American Society of Newspaper Editors and the Society of Professional Journalists (SPJ) or company-wide codes of media groups. Nonetheless, conspicuous by its absence in the four standards offered in this article is the principle of truth telling, the first principle of the SPJ code (Black, Steele, & Barney, 1999) and one articulated well by Lambeth (1992) in shaping "an Eclectic System of Journalism Ethics" (pp. 24–27). Four of his widely quoted five principles of truth telling, humaneness, justice, freedom, and stewardship of free expression—all but truth telling—can be accommodated within one or more of this article's standards of respect, accountability, and avoidance of self-deception.

Although Christians and Traber (1997) identified truth telling as the first of four universal values, truth telling simply does not fare as well in this article. Perhaps it is for idiosyncratic reasons—which include considering journalists as reporters rather than truth tellers. Therefore a bit more discussion is required as to why truth telling is not included in this article's list of supposed universal ethical standards. It is not sufficient to say that Lambeth (1992) and Christians and Traber already have made a compelling case for truth telling and it need not be reiterated here—even though that is the case.

Certainly, ethical behavior requires us to stretch. Ethical standards are goals more than they are habits. But generally we can be accountable if we want; we can respect others if we but make the effort; and introspection can offset self-deception. Sometimes, however, we cannot tell the truth even when we desperately want to because we don't know what it is. Perhaps that is reading too much into the principle of truth telling, but Bok's (1979) distinction between *telling the truth* and *being truthful* was persuasive. Bok (1979) opted for "being truthful," or for truthfulness: Being truthful meant sharing what you believe to be accurate information. "Telling the truth" had troubling connotations because, among other things, we may not know what the truth is; people who are convinced they have the truth have done horrible things to those they consider to be in error, and sometimes people use truth telling to hurt others.

This perspective is guilty of thinking of the concept of truth telling as more than being honest and trying to be as accurate as humanly possible in the reporting of the human condition. The idea of turning to the local paper or to television news for truth telling is not a comfortable concept for at least the following reasons.

As noted earlier, this article defines journalism somewhat narrowly in terms of a news orientation. That news orientation differs from communication settings that are interpersonal in nature and more amenable to "truth telling" discussions, perhaps because the participants in an interpersonal setting may be on more equal footing to evaluate information given and received than is the case, say, with Dan Rather's network news audience.

---

*Journalists ... reduce the degree
to which audiences are misled.*

Almost all we know about news gathering and news reporting speaks to how fraught with potential error those processes are. Live coverage compounds the problem as news audiences accompany reporters down blind alleys. Reporters are not so much oriented toward telling the truth as they are toward reducing the degree to which they and the news audience are misled. Efforts to be honest and accurate—or, efforts to not intentionally deceive—seem fairer measures of the ethics of news reporting than does truth telling.

In that spirit, perhaps the ethical newspaper should carry a warning label or warranty:

The contents of today's newspaper should be treated with care. The information collected and presented was done so under circumstances and conditions that, history has shown, are error prone. The newsroom budget and funds available to help assure accuracy are

constrained by the corporation's fiduciary responsibility to stock-
holders. Consequently, the reader is advised to seek multiple sources
of information and to be sure to read the paper tomorrow for any corrections or clarifications or for new developments needed to put today's news into perspective. Although we cannot warranty that all
information in today's paper is accurate, we do warranty that our editors and staff practice no intentional deception, and we do abide by
an affirmative duty to publish corrections promptly and fully.

Having explained why truth telling is not in this article's list, two caveats are needed: (a) Some version of truth telling is likely to appear in any final list of "universals" because it speaks to what the audience expects,
rightfully or not, of journalists, and truth telling may, after all, be short
hand for the journalist's efforts to be accurate and honest. (b) Having
closed the front door to "truth telling," at least in this article, it is not the in-
tent to treat "knowing thyself" as "truth telling" in different clothes. A distinction is drawn between being truthful with oneself and being truthful
with others—just as it is drawn between privacy and openness—although
the two are related and, as suggested previously, one needs to be honest
with oneself as a condition of being honest with others.

Having digressed to explain why truth telling is not included in the list
of universal standards, we now consider more fully those that are.

Applications to Journalism: Perspectives on the Four Standards

Use Restraint: Violence should never be the first resort in conflict
                  resolution.

Neither *violence* nor *violent* are found in the news-oriented codes of the
American Society of Newspaper Editors or the SPJ. Yet news reporting historically and theoretically has instrumental value among those seeking
nonviolent resolution of social conflicts. As president of Washington Col-
lege, Robert E. Lee looked to law, journalism, and other disciplines to help
rebuild the South and to provide alternatives to the violence of war, according to Lee biographers and Washington and Lee University, renamed
in Lee's honor.

First Amendment theorist Thomas I. Emerson (1970) recognized the
"safety-valve" nature of the Amendment:

Freedom of expression thus provides a framework in which the conflict necessary to the progress of a society can take place without destroying the soci-

ety. It is an essential mechanism for maintaining the balance between stability and change. (p. 7)

A universal ethical standard that abhors violence as a first resort is unworkable unless there is concomitant recognition of the need for open discussion and the accompanying journalistic culture as appropriate, necessary alternatives.

On a less global scale, the standard against violence as a first resort counsels patience to the journalist in coverage and commentary on controversial, perhaps explosive, community issues. Historically and theoretically, the standard must be part of a journalistic ethic, if only to suggest what journalism can contribute to its society.

Know thyself: Self-deception—lying to oneself—is not a healthy practice for an individual or for a society.

Journalists often pride themselves on matters of integrity and self-awareness. Critics routinely are told that no profession is as introspective. In such declarations journalists typically have reference to their endless conversations about how a news story was or was not covered or should have been covered. But to "know thyself" and to avoid "self-deception" require more than being candid about one's mistakes.

For example, Merrill (1996) wrote the following:

Self-deception, for the existentialist, is the greatest vice, for it robs man of his personhood, his integrity; it deludes him into thinking that he is nothing more than a robot having an essence pushed upon him by *outside* forces. Man *makes himself,* says the existentialist, or defines what he is in the course of choosing, acting, and existing. (p. 34)

Self-deception by the journalist can also corrupt the news audience. The audience relies upon reporters to somehow avoid the human tendency to know what they are looking for and, *voila,* they discover and report evidence to support their self-deception.

For the journalist, the pressures for deceiving oneself as well as a sometimes willing news audience come from within and without. Forget about the corporate powers and pressures that have been well-documented (Cranberg, Bezanson, & Soloski, 2001); think about the sports fan who expects the local paper to support the potential and the prowess of the hometown football team, regardless of evidence to the contrary.

The concept of news judgment requires that editors and reporters be aware of their predilections so they can make story evaluations and word

choices based on the significance of a news event and not on their biases or
the drive to hype a story.

Social psychologist Erich Fromm (1966) also linked self-awareness and
being a good reporter:

> To be able to listen to oneself is a prerequisite for the ability to listen to others; to
> be at home with oneself is the necessary condition for relating to others. (p. 113)

For these and other reasons, the universal ethic of "Know thyself" must
have a place in universal standards for journalists. As the laws of physics
can be ignored or dismissed only at one's peril, so it is when we kid ourselves on personal matters. Unfortunately, while journalists pay considerable attention to concerns regarding the deception of others in the reporting process, concerns with self-deception do not fare as well.

Respect others: Do not abuse one's authority or stewardship.

Principles of respect and stewardship are inherent in ethical relations
and articulated in the Golden Rule teachings of Confucius, Christ, and others. For our immediate purposes, we focus on concerns for the weaker
party and Eric Fromm's (1966) perspective on *respect*. Relevant here, too, is
the Kantian maxim that we treat people as ends, not as objects or means.

Fromm (1966) advised that the journalist's concept of objectivity has
more to do with "respect" of another's point of view than with detachment
or disinterest. Perhaps we disagree with a view, but generally we can respect a person's right to hold such an opinion and be able to faithfully report his reasons for doing so. Fromm stated,

> Objectivity is not, as it is often implied in a false idea of "scientific" objectiv-
> ity, synonymous with detachment, with absence of interest and care. How
> can one penetrate the veiling surface of things to their causes and relation-
> ships if one does not have an interest that is vital and sufficiently impelling
> for so laborious a task? (p. 111)

As suggested earlier, ethical standards seldom call for or demand respect for authority or for those in position of power (although they certainly do not forbid it). The concern is more with stewardship, of not abus-
ing one's own authority, power, or influence.

Risks of abuse are high when people become subjects of news stories in
unwanted or unexpected situations. Consider tapes of 911 telephone calls.
In panic, an individual calls 911, seeking help in what often is the most trau-
matic experience of the person's life. However, the audiotape and transcript

of the call may be a public record, readily available for broadcast on that evening's television news or for reprinting in the next day's newspaper.

Needed perspective? Or harm to a victim?

Journalists say such coverage provides the audience with a needed perspective on an incident of community concern and also holds public agencies accountable for their responses. Perhaps. Most people, however, have heard enough such rebroadcasts to know that public agencies usually respond in competent fashion. It is questionable just what needed perspective is provided by exploiting the anguish of the victim or witness. Locally, on the anniversary of a tragedy, a television station replayed the unsettling 911 telephone call a woman made seconds before she drowned as her car sunk in a rain-filled quarry. The tape was rebroadcast as part of a story on safe driving in bad weather!

In less dramatic events, respect is illustrated in its most simplistic form in getting the other side of the story and in being fair in treatment of news sources. This principle might be carried an additional step when the reporter anticipates the criticism a source may be subjected to as a result of news coverage and gives the source an opportunity to respond even before the criticism is raised.

For example, a local newspaper several years ago had a story about "young love." Why the paper gave the story the treatment it did is puzzling. Nonetheless, the story dealt with two high school students, both in their teens, neither particularly bright, and both sort of social outcasts and from dysfunctional or broken homes. Nonetheless they found each other, and their love resulted in the premature birth of triplets. By the time the third infant had died, the medical bills were approaching $500,000, presumably to be paid by public funds. But the couple still professed love for one another.

That was the essence of the story. Surely, in keeping with the standard of respect and stewardship, the reporter should have anticipated some of the obvious reactions to such pathos. All the reporter needed to say to the girl and boy was, "You know, some people are going to be upset with you and wonder how or why so much money should be spent because of what you did. What would you say to these people? How would you answer them?"

However, as it was, in the "young love" story, the reporter and the paper just left the couple to fend for themselves. The naive couple seemed to relish the attention they were getting before the reactions set in. They soon broke up.

If a news reporter is going to lay bare the lives of the vulnerable, it would seem ethical to provide the vulnerable with a measure of protection from exploitation or with the opportunity to defend themselves.

The standard of respect is faithful to at least the first half of the axiom that it is the journalist's duty to comfort the afflicted and afflict the comfortable.

Be accountable: One bears responsibility for the consequences of one's
                  actions.

Given much of the preceding discussion, perhaps the question is not whether journalists should be accountable, but rather what should they be accountable for, to whom should they be accountable, and who holds them accountable?

If the focus is on what journalists are accountable for, these five concepts of the Commission on the Freedom of the Press (1947) remain as good a baseline as any. The commission's litany held that the press should be accountable for providing as follows:

A truthful, comprehensive, and intelligent account of the day's events in a context that gives them meaning.

A forum for the exchange of comment and criticism.

The projection of a representative picture of the constituent groups in the society.

The presentation and clarification of the goals and values of the society.

Full access to the day's intelligence.

Regarding accountability, Bonhoeffer (1971), the theologian, wrote as follows:

The man who feels neither responsibility towards the past nor desire to shape the future is one who "forgets," and I don't know how one can really get at such a person and bring him to his senses. (p. 203)

Regarding the two questions (a) To whom is accountability owed? and (b) Who holds one accountable? as troubling as the shorthand answers may be, when we come to ethical concerns, the answers seem to be (a) others and (b) self.

Conclusions

The quest for universal ethical standards in journalism is worthwhile and may be productive. This article has advanced four general standards that can be applied across cultures and across ethical schools of thought. The standards also have relevance for the day-to-day practice of journalism. However, the ethical anguish inherent in that day-to-day practice will not be eliminated even if there is agreement on what universal standards should shape decisions. Agreement on some ethical anchors, however, would be a giant step away from the "it-all-depends" mentality.

In further consideration of these issues, more time could profitably be spent in looking at both truth telling and self-deception as to their utility in helping understand what journalists are and should be about. Certainly it would be helpful if, in discussions of truth telling as a universal principle, authors would make it clear that what they have in mind is more in terms of being honest than in issuing infallible pronouncements.

Inherent in our quest is the irony of seeking the universal while recognizing that perhaps it can only be found or realized ultimately in the individual. Kant captured the irony in this passage from his *Critique of Pure Reason:*

> Two things fill the mind with ever new and increasing admiration and awe … the starry heavens above and the moral law within. (quoted by Leslie, 2000, p. 76)

Notes

1. The organizations included the International Organization of Journalists, the International Federation of Journalists, the International Catholic Union of the Press, the Latin American Federation of Journalists, the Federation of Arab Journalists, the Union of African Journalists, and the Confederation of ASEAN Journalists.
2. In discussions such as this, participants often invoke the physicians' dictum of *Primum non nocere.* The "first do no harm" credo in medicine, however, typically deals with physical effects (but allows amputations, of course) and not with information sharing. When it comes to what information should be shared with a patient and the family and when it should be shared, physicians can be as "at sea" as journalists and *Primum non nocere* is not a panacea.

References

Berlin, I. (1980). *The crooked timber of humanity, chapters in the history of ideas.* New York: Knopf.

Black, J., Steele, B., & Barney, R. (1999). Doing ethics in journalism (3rd ed.). Needham Heights, MA: Allyn & Bacon.

Bok, S. (1979). *Lying, moral choice in public and private life.* New York: Vintage.

Bonhoeffer, D. (1963). *Ethics.* New York: Macmillan.

Bonhoeffer, D. (1971). *Letters and papers from prison, the enlarged edition.* New York: Macmillan.

Christians, C., & Traber, M. (Eds). (1997). *Communication ethics and universal values.* Thousand Oaks, CA: Sage.

Commission on Freedom of the Press. (1947). *A free and responsible press.* Chicago: University of Chicago Press.

Cranberg, G., Bezanson, R., & Soloski, J. (2001). *Taking stock: Journalism and the publicly traded newspaper company.* Ames: Iowa State University Press.

Emerson, T. (1970). *The system of freedom of expression.* New York: Vintage.

Fromm, E. (1966). *Man for himself: An inquiry into the psychology of ethics.* New York: Holt.

Lambeth, E. (1992). *Committed journalism: An ethic for the profession* (2nd ed.). Bloomington and Indianapolis: University of Indiana Press.

Leslie, L. (2000). *Mass communication ethics.* Boston: Houghton Mifflin.

Many voices one world, Report by the International Commission for the Study of Communication Problems. (1980). London: Kogan Page; New York, Unesco, Paris/In association with World Association for Christian Communication, London. (Reprinted 1988).

Merrill, J. (1989). *The dialectic in journalism.* Baton Rouge: Louisiana State University Press.

Merrill, J. (1994). *The legacy of wisdom.* Ames: Iowa State University Press.

Merrill, J. (1996). *Existential journalism.* Ames: Iowa State University Press.

Saunders, K. (1934). *The ideals of East and West.* New York: Macmillan.

Wiener, P. (Ed.). (1974). *Dictionary of the history of ideas, Vol. 1–4.* New York: Scribners.

Journal of Mass Media Ethics, 17(4), 277–289

A Universal Code of Journalism Ethics: Problems, Limitations, and Proposals

Roberto Herrscher
Les Heures University of Barcelona, Spain

❏ *As the worlds of economics, politics, culture, and communications face a growing wave of globalization that will likely continue, ethical challenges for journalists have also gone global. I propose a clear division between ethics codes for media owners, the public, and professional journalists and present a set of considerations and specific rules applicable only to the last group. In this article I advocate a universal code of journalistic ethics but point out problems and warn against dangers that have made the application of such codes difficult in the past. A universal code should consider the voluntary nature of such an endeavor, the cultural and economic differences in various journalistic traditions, and the problem of producing solutions acceptable to all involved.*

Is a universal code of ethics possible in the world of journalism of the early 21st century? Is it desirable? These and other questions arise whenever a group of journalists or communication scholars gather to discuss the possibility—and possible contents—of a Universal Code of Ethics for our profession. This brief article will leave these questions open, but will try to elaborate on some points that seem to be important for the debate. It is a personal position, but I believe it expresses some of the doubts and a few of the certainties that have been circulating in Spain and Latin America over the past decade.

Few activities pose so many questions as journalism when it comes to codes of ethics. Lawyers or physicians have no need of discussing what and who is a lawyer or a doctor. Journalists do. Teachers and professors can more easily separate what is public and what is private in their work and their lives. Journalists cannot. For public servants, most practices that are ethically wrong are also illegal. Not so in the world of mass media.

We must also start every discussion within the context of many years and many attempts at elaborating codes capable of improving the ethical standards of journalists and media, and the service they render to their communities. Historians trace the first formal codes of ethics in the beginning of the

20th century. They have existed in good and bad times, in times of pride and in times of shame. In Argentina, during the 1976–1983 military dictatorship, journalists had a code of ethics. That did not prevent them from rejecting the Mothers of Plaza de Mayo who came to newsrooms begging for someone to publish news about the 30,000 people who disappeared around the country. It was "not news" (Blaustein & Zubieta, 2000).

At present, codes of ethics there are aplenty. One of the most complete collections, by the Mexican scholar Ernesto Villanueva (1999), lists 89, seven by international bodies and regional assemblies and federations of journalists, 15 by individual media, and the rest by national or provincial bodies.

> *What can we expect of a code*
> *that has no judges, police, or*
> *prisons to enforce it?*

Most look ethical and professional enough, but it is hard to guess from them which countries and regions have the most democratic, sophisticated, and independent media. Some of the worst dictatorships of the 20th century have copied and enhanced Western-style constitutions that look perfect on paper.

If a constitution, mandatory for citizens of the state it rules, can become such a collection of lies and hypocrisies as that of Italy under Mussolini or Paraguay under General Stroessner, what can we expect of a code that has no judges, no police, and no prisons to enforce it? In a way, and taking the argument to its absurd extreme, it is like trying to concoct a law against burglary that robbers would accept, or a moral code for society to the liking of Giacomo Casanova.

Hence my first hypothesis: To be accepted, recognized as valid, and followed (at least sometimes), a journalistic code of ethics must take in consideration the general ideas and concepts of ethics that are actually prevalent within the journalistic world (journalists, owners, managers) and the real conditions under which collection and presentation of news takes place in today's newsrooms.

Who Is the Subject?

Different codes have different subjects in mind. Some mention their goals explicitly while others do not, but no code was designed for all those in the mass communication process: individual journalists, media owners, the public as news consumers, and citizens who want their messages known.

This is, I think, the central difference between the codes of ethics of media organizations and their international institutions, and those penned by federations of journalists.

We are talking here of three inter-related but different sets of rights:

- Freedom of the press, as established, for example, in the First Amendment of the U.S. Constitution, is basically a right of the *owner of a media company* (the "press").
- Free speech is the right of a *journalist* or anybody who wants to tell something to others. Sometimes free speech by a journalist can conflict with her owner's freedom to suppress, change, or manipulate what the journalist wants to say.
- Freedom of information belongs to *the citizen*. It is the citizens' right to know what is happening in the public sphere, to receive a variety of positions and voices, and to be treated as discerning adults.

In a recent example, different actors viewed these rights as one and the same, but each spoke of his or her own right. In 2001 the Costa Rican National Assembly discussed a new Press Law for the country.

The Association of Professional Journalists (*Colegio de Periodistas*) presented a draft law, but the media directors presented an alternative. In each, the subjects differ, even when points are similar. The journalists' proposal includes the *right of conscience* of media workers to have their intellectual works and professional criteria respected. It is, in a way, a right against the media directors. The directors meld companies and journalists, with rights protecting them both from interference, control, or attack from outsiders: the government or other sources of power.

And who protects the citizen at the receiving end of the news? Rivers and Mathews (1988) concluded their study with a survey of the institution of the Ombudsman, called "defender of the reader" (*Defensor del Lector*) in Spanish language media.

In many newspapers, it is the ombudsman who decides whether reporters and editors have complied with the paper's code of ethics in cases in which their conduct comes under debate. However, as appointees of the organization, ombudsmen have usually been much more effective when dealing with ethical questions raised by the behavior of individual journalists than when the problem comes from the editorial policy of the organization.

Proposed Values for the Code

This is a short list of principles that might be included in a universal code of ethics. It is proposed especially for journalists as subjects of rights and obligations.

1. The first has to do with *truth*. Most journalists agree that it is important to make clear whether an event has happened. Some questions are a matter of opinion or taste, but many of the events about which the journalist writes or speaks are facts. Even in the midst of postmodern deconstruction of certainty in the truths of science and religion, still reports of some events are true while others may not be. The role of the journalist is to find out what has actually happened and to tell it with precision and clarity. There is no end to the debate between those who defend the possibility and desirability of objectivity and those who say it is unattainable (Tuchman, 1972). But most codes, in one way or another, state that some events are facts and some are not, and journalists should be able to show their publics the difference.

2. The second issue has to do with *completeness*. No story is complete if journalists know they have (or can gather) more information that is relevant, important, or necessary for understanding the situation. A half truth is in part a lie. Journalists may select arguments, quotes, and material that fit well with their general hypothesis, ignoring what does not. The information must be complete, and, as with most other such principles, each case must be analyzed individually to see how this can be achieved. I would place the powerful dictum "to tell the truth, all the truth, and nothing but the truth" at the core of a Universal Code of Journalistic Ethics.

An ever-increasing difficulty in separating news from ads.

---

3. The third principle has to do with *conflict of interests*. Journalists cannot have personal interest in the causes, businesses, or parties of their sources. Neither should a news organization cover the activities of its owner, affiliates, allies, or rivals as news. Since that principle is impossible to comply with, because the public of that medium would suffer the loss of a piece of news that might be important, the principle should be that relationships between the owners and sources or characters in stories has to be made known to the public.

4. The fourth is related to *freedom, independence, and self-esteem*, but it has links to the previous one. As journalists in the Spanish-speaking world come more and more from universities where they study a magma of courses shared by people interested in journalism, public relations, and publicity, it is more and more difficult to instill in new professionals the "journalistic approach" toward the world. There is an ever-growing difficulty in separating the world of news from the world of ads, and in this context I believe the journalist has a central role in building a voice radi-

cally different from that of the propagandist and PR official. A universal code of journalistic ethics should push journalists and media to build relationships in which the integrity, independence, and professional criteria of the journalist and the interest of the public in receiving an impartial (if not objective) account are respected.

5. The fifth pertains to *honesty* as a value in the central relationship in the process of communication: that of journalists and their publics. Publics have a right to know how the information was collected and why the medium or the journalist in question considers it important and relevant in cases in which absence of that information leaves the story incomplete.

6. The sixth has to do with the *respect of privacy and honor*. Journalists do not have a right to publish a fact for the sole reason that is has happened. Private people have a right to demand and obtain privacy for their private lives, and even public figures have a right to privacy in a more limited sphere. If it does not affect public interest, private actions should not be published if those involved ask that it remain private.

7. The seventh principle would deal with the *treatment of ethnic groups, sexes, minorities, religious and sexual persuasions, and other groups* that are seen as different in the society where the journalist is working. It is easier to state that these groups and their members should be treated fairly than to determine what that means. For the journalist, all people are equal. The easiest experiment is to see if an article about a woman, an Indian, a gay man, or a Muslim would be written in the same way if it dealt with a White, Protestant, straight man.

"Deciding What's News"

Herbert Gans' (1980) book studied how two news magazines and two television news programs decided which of the millions of events and pseudoevents that come their way every day are transformed into stories. If most of what happens never becomes material for the journalist to work on, the discussion on how that fragment that does is usually only a small part of the debate.

The history of world media is replete with silences: Many political massacres, domestic crimes, and cruel injustices have not been deemed news by media organizations.

They simply were not treated at all. In some media AIDS was not news during the first years of the disease. In the prestigious newspapers of the first half of the 19th century, slavery or inferior rights for women were not issues.

A code of ethics should discuss the definition of news and the way in which each medium and each society defines it. A journalistic profession serving its society and presenting what happens in its midst with accuracy and completeness should not leave important and relevant events or developments untreated. It is up to each society to discuss which issues are important. This would add an eighth principle to the list:

8. This eighth principle would deal with *importance and relevance*. Of course journalists should be allowed to write or broadcast banal or superficial news. If not, thousands would be without a job. But the journalistic profession as a whole should see to it that the fundamental issues in the public life of the society it serves are dealt with in the media.

Compulsory Versus Voluntary

Now who will make sure this or any other code is respected?

Doctors can expel a fellow physician from the profession and ban him or her from practicing medicine. Journalists cannot, even if they wanted to. The closest they can get is professional ostracism, the type of punishment that fell over *Washington Post* reporter Janet Cooke after her cocaine-addicted boy Jimmy was discovered to be her invention. Her action was clearly seen as passing the limits that practicing journalists of the time wanted their profession to respect.

Laws also change according to the morality of the times. Slavery, torture, inferior rights for women, and disregard of the environment were once accepted socially and legally all over the world.

In the case of ethics codes with no legal enforcement muscle, like those regarding journalists and media, one of the first points to discuss is the three aspects of respect and authority contained in any code:

1. The degree to which *the rules* themselves are seen as representing standards the profession considers ethically valuable.
2. The prestige, independence, and representivity of the body *that discusses, writes and approves* the code and its individual members.
3. The prestige, independence, and representivity of the organ and individuals entrusted with the *application* of the code in concrete cases.

---

*More difficult to agree on draftors
with international respect.*

It is very difficult to attain all three at a national or regional level. Much more difficult is to agree on a body of journalistic legislators, judges, and laws that command international respect and are seen as representing the ideas and values of journalists and media organizations in widely different cultures and settings.

The problem is compounded by the other legitimacy question of a code of ethics: social legitimacy, a new (sometimes linked, sometimes not) set of sources of authority. Principles, authors, and appliers of the journalistic code must also be accepted by social groups and leaders to lend the code legitimacy outside the world of journalists. In some countries, military codes are accepted and obeyed by the officers, but social forces outside the regiment walls may see them as self-serving justifications of crimes and errors.

A code of journalistic ethics must have among its main effects the growth of responsibility of journalists and media toward the society that they serve. If the code is to be effective, nonjournalists should see it as a tool with which they can challenge and change bad journalistic practices. If outsiders see a certain code and its enforcers as a means of justifying whatever is done in the trade, the code is a failure, no matter how well meaning and well written are its articles.

Who Controls Information?

Historically, only the Rights of Man of the French Revolution and the Universal Declaration of Human Rights adopted by the United Nations came anywhere close to universal knowledge and acceptance. And still today, millions of humans are denied those rights by states that give lip service to the principles of human rights.

Governments around the globe speak of human rights but think (not always hypocritically, they genuinely think) that only their citizens, their group, their tribe, the members of their religion have human rights. They think that rights were created and should be used to protect their own. For all others, what applies is the right of war. When the enemy has not yet attacked, it is right to prevent the occurrence of the attack that the enemy no doubt has in mind. Acceptance of the same rights for all is an exception in the history of the human race (Dyson, 1984).

In the field of communication, there is also a history of our rights versus your rights. During the second half of the 20th century, government agencies, journalistic and news business organizations, and academics from the United States and other Western states have linked the free flow of information, the right to establish and operate private news companies, and the freedom to obtain and publish news without government control, to the idea of democracy. They have promoted all three as one and the same right in the Third World. The West, that is to say, has aggressively pursued a line of thought that linked personal freedom and political liberty to boundless action by news companies, presenting them as three sides of the same good: the Free World.

Free speech and free information may be better served in this Western tradition than in the Soviet system of information, but boundless, limitless rights for the powerful news companies is not part of the same right, and can sometimes violate it. When a media giant becomes a multimedia monopoly or oligopoly, the right of the citizen to listen to different and comparatively powerful voices from diverging sides in the social divide is not served. One voice is strong, and it becomes stronger still when there are no limits to its power.

> *A strong voice becomes
> stronger when there
> are no limits to its power.*

In socialist countries, of course, the press was (and still is in the couple of surviving examples) an obedient server of the political power, which in turn was presented as a true representative of the poor, the workers, the people in their fight for liberation. In the Soviet Union, Eastern Europe, Socialist Africa, North Korea, Vietnam, and Cuba, the result was economic and social guarantees for the people, and media that cannot be seen as anything but propaganda. Probably no social group suffered more from the stiffness and authoritarianism of Communist thought than the journalists.

But, at present, when Communist ideals and practices are ridiculed in one paragraph in manuals for journalists, I think it is important to stop and think why they exercised such a strong appeal for many prominent professors, journalists, and government agencies from the Third World. What was the lure of a system that produced *Pravda* or *Granma* for young rebels who dreamt of equality and freedom for all?

I think it was the problem that still lies at the core of the communication system developed by the great democracies, the capitalistic West. In most Third World countries, powerful companies that run the elite newspapers, radio stations, and television networks are both members and allies of the economic, social, and political establishment. In Latin American universities we always saw at much closer range the ills of local media, which disguised their true functions as allies of political powers that often included military dictatorships as service to the public, than the obvious and usually ridiculous shortcomings and criminal cronyism of the Cuban or East German press (Mattelart & Mattelart, 1988).

The Chomsky and Herman (1988) theory of four filters in which media owners, advertisers, establishment sources, and their flak effect combine influences to ensure a pro-establishment, pro-business version of each story prevails in the media is still seen as relevant in various parts of the world. The mass media as organizations say they represent the public good and the private citizen, but through innumerable actions and omissions, they are seen to represent the views and interests of the establishment. Many newspapers, radio, and TV news programs do work for the common citizen as well, but not only and not always. They are better than they could be, but worse than they say they are.

And there are large and expanding international media corporations that buy more and more news companies and other business and, in an alarming proportion, cover as news the activities of their owners, their allies, or their competition (Hazen & Winokur, 1997). From the South, when the giant media conglomerates speak of "freedom of the press," many critics hear instead, "our freedom to do business."

So far, globalization has brought more richness to the world, but the distribution of money, welfare, and power is as unequal as ever. Representatives of big companies may impose a universal code on journalists around the world. But it has the danger of becoming nothing but the expression of the current situation: a line of discourse in which freedom of expression is deliberately mixed up with free hands for that 10% of the World population that controls 80% of its riches.

Universalism Versus Cultural Relativism

Different countries and different groups inside them definitely require different media and differing relationships with their journalists. U.S. professors of journalism who have ventured to the four corners of the World to teach locals how to do their job better have often tried to impose the style, priorities, agenda, and language of, for example, *The New York Times* to newsrooms in Hungary, Kenya, or Nicaragua. They have met with a fierce reaction and bitter resentment. A successful journalistic operation grows from the culture, values, and expectations of its own society. However, those professors and trainers who traveled with an open mind, trying to instill principles and help foreign media grow within their own system of meanings and values, conquered hearts and won battles against authoritarianism and ignorance.

Not all media and not all journalists should work in the same manner and write in the same style. But there is a core list of principles that can be adopted internationally. It is the list I propose in the third section of this article. For me, a universal code of ethics is indeed desirable and attainable. It would help solve the problems created by governments, economic groups, and journalists around the world who hide behind ideas of *cultural relativ-*

ism to defend communication systems that keep them in power and the people in ignorance.

Fernando Savater (1978) posed eloquently the problem of the shady undemocratic regimes that—pretending to defend local traditions, national culture, and sovereignty—are really defending the authoritarian clinging to power of a local elite, the repression of opposition, and their own reaction to modernization and change.

> Human rights were invented by Europe, but now they belong to all and they must be imposed for the sake of humanity. The Latin American Indians had no concept like our human rights, but now they defend these rights against their white oppressors. These rights have become universal. In that context, I believe in ethical imperialism. Some Africans cut the clitoris of little girls and say it is their tradition, their culture, their right. No, it isn't. Local traditions must be allowed to go as far as the point when they crash against the wall of human rights. And then they must stop. (Savater, personal communication, April 1989)

Objectivity, a curtain behind which the media hide.

Can some principles in the field of communication become universal in this same way? Even for those of us who think the answer is yes, it is difficult to pinpoint the specific principles that would make such a list. McQuail (1992) said that objectivity is a principle that journalists around the world share. But a survey of national codes of ethics shows that, in many countries, objectivity is considered unattainable and even a curtain behind which the media hide their true colors (Villanueva, 1999).

The balance between respect and practice of freedom of information as a human right and respect and understanding of different cultural practices and traditions must be a permanent concern of journalists and cannot be solved by a general rule that can automatically tell us what to do in each case. The first rule regarding cultural identities is to acknowledge their existence and importance, and to give a voice and a space to different ways of looking at life and its particulars.

Sometimes it is hard to accept journalistic traditions of other countries. The Japanese, for example, traditionally treat their authorities with reverence. A U.S. journalist would feel such a tradition deprives journalists and their public of a basic, universal function of the trade: the watchdog function. Japanese media are in fact changing, but due to long, deep social changes in their own social fabric, not by the imposition of a Western-style universal code.

But a Spanish journalist would as easily feel perplexed by some practices in U.S. media, like the tradition of endorsing candidates on the editorial page for elected positions. Treating all candidates fairly after the official endorsement is something Latin journalists do not see themselves (or anybody!) capable of doing.

If these differences are acknowledged and journalists from different countries and traditions learn to become more open and less arrogant, the richness of the colorful picture of world journalism can make a universal code of ethics possible. Since those differences do not affect the core values of our profession, I think they make the agreement on a common ground more necessary and more useful.

A Code for All Seasons?

In times of war, disaster, national mourning, or public jubilation, the media usually suspend their role as watchdog or their quest for objectivity and do what they believe is required: participate in the national or social sentiment, lead, soothe, inspire, exult, shout, or cry. Dayan and Katz (1994) called these occurrences media events.

In these moments, when so many media owners, editors, and reporters suspend the standards of their daily work, it may be more important than ever to stick to solid ethical principles. The public is listening with special attention and tend to respond with actions to what they read and hear.

An ethical code is designed to stay valid under all circumstances. I think it is important to discuss the possibility of a code for all seasons in the face of politicians, social leaders, and even journalists who change their ethical standards according to the moment. It need not be a national disaster. In the Spanish-speaking world, the most objective media show their partisan nature during electoral campaigns. The most serious newspapers day after day start placing their preferred candidate on their front page, their magazine, and their pages of lifestyles.

As I write this article, the TV set blasts the latest news about the terrorist attacks on New York and Washington. How should the U.S. media cover such national tragedies? A truly universal code should be valid even today, September 11, 2001. Especially today.

Conclusion

The objective behind this article is the desire to bring forth some questions I think should be taken into consideration when discussing the possibility of a universal code of ethics for the journalistic profession. I also wanted to present some of the problems I see regarding the possible contents of such a code.

Even when journalistic traditions and the cultures in which they develop are widely different in some aspects, I believe that discussion of a possible universal code in the academic sphere can be useful, positive, and healthy for all those involved.

Given the power and influence of journalism and its capacity to shape ideas, values, metaphors, and myths in the social minds of almost all the world's communities today, the discussion of such a code is also a necessity. Communication is becoming more and more global. Since its practices, codes, and vices are becoming more and more homogeneous in the five continents, it is a necessity to try to bring high ethical standards and spread them to the centers and corners in which journalists strive.

I still do not know if a universal code of journalistic ethics is possible. But in the process of elaborating this article I conclude that, provided that cultural, political, social, and economic differences are acknowledged, it can do as much good as a universal declaration of human rights. Human rights are still violated, but without the declaration the world would be much worse off.

Throughout the world there are examples of positive developments due to the adoption of codes of ethics by individual media, regional or national associations of journalists, or groupings of media owners. Open discussion of a possible code is already in itself an important step. Moreso, a debate on a universal one. Communication and information have become global, whether we like it or not. A global code of ethics is the logical consequence of change in the way we work as journalists and receive information as citizens and consumers.

Many aspects have to be taken into consideration, and the challenge is big, but as the power and effect of mass media grow, the need for a journalistic code of ethics is seen as more useful and important than ever.

References

Blaustein, E., & Zubieta, M. (2000). *Decíamos ayer. La prensa argentina durante el proceso.* Buenos Aires, Argentina: Editorial Colihue.

Chomsky, N., & Herman, E. (1988). *Manufacturing consent.* New York: Pantheon.

Dayan, D., & Katz, E. (1994). *Eventos mediáticos* [Media events. The live broadcasting of history]. México: Fondo de Cultura Económica.

Dyson, F. (1984). *Armas y esperanza* [Weapons and hope]. México: Fondo de Cultura Económica.

Gans, H. (1980). *Deciding what's news.* New York: Vintage.

Hazen, D., & Winokur, J. (1997). *We the media. A citizen's guide to fighting for media democracy.* New York: New Press.

Mattelart, A., & Mattelart, M. (1988). *Pensar sobre los medios*. Comunicación y Crítica Social. Costa Rica: Departmento Ecuménico de Investigaciones.

McQuail, D. (1992). *La acción de los medios. Los medios de comunicación y el interés público* [Media performance. Mass communication and the public interest]. Buenos Aires, Argentina: Amorrortu.

Rivers, W., & Mathews, C. (1988). *La ética en los medios de comunicación* [Ethics for the media]. México: Gernika.

Savater, F. (1978). *Perdonadme, ortodoxos*. Madrid, Spain: Alianza Editorial.

Tuchman, G. (1972). *La objetividad como ritual estratégico*. CIC #4 (originally published in the *American Journal of Sociology*)

Villanueva, E. (1999). *Deontología Informativa. Códigos deontológicos de la prensa escrita en el mundo*. Ciudad de México, México: Universidad Iberoamericana.

Journal of Mass Media Ethics, 17(4), 290–303

Journalism After September 11: Unity as Moral Imperative

Dennis D. Cali
East Carolina University

❏ *Following the terrorist attacks of September 11, 2001, journalism in the United States changed. Journalistic norms of objectivity and distance opened to a participatory mode of reporting. A communitarian journalism emerged in which journalists became "at one" with their subjects as they lived the story they were reporting. Chiara Lubich of Italy presents a philosophical foundation for this journalistic approach, proposing "unity" as the ethic that should guide mass media communicators. In this essay I review Lubich's moral perspective and consider its implications for media ethics.*

Marshall McLuhan's "global village" quaked on September 11, 2001, as terror attacks on New York and Washington ignited a new awareness of multi-layered discord in the global community. Televised reports of those atrocities, together with continual reports of terror across the world, were graphic reminders of deep fractures in the human family. But equally graphic were media portrayals of an emergent post-9/11 unity. Especially in the first days after September 11, the mass media lionized ordinary heroism within America's national family, giving ubiquitous and unprecedented attention to public and private acts of compassion and solidarity.

This new, unifying journalism has persisted since September 11, 2001, leading journalists to reflect on changes that have occurred in journalistic norms. This essay identifies those changes as communitarian and considers the moral theory formulated by Chiara Lubich of Italy as a philosophical foundation for them. For more than 60 years as leader of the Focolare Movement, an international communitarian organization that promotes civic and religious unity, Lubich has urged people in religious and civic structures to live for one another and to make themselves one with their neighbor. (*Focolare*, which is Italian for "hearth," conveys the sentiment of unity felt when people gather around the family fireplace.) Lubich poses her communitarian moral ethic as a normative ethic capable of guiding communication practice across the globe and of helping to unite the global village.

Journalism's "New Normal"

In the days immediately after September 11, 2001, a shocked and griev-ing media devoted extensive attention to the goodness with which Ameri-cans reacted to the terror attacks on New York and Washington. *The Pitts-burgh Post-Gazette*, for example, ran a story about an ironworker's voluntary decision to take his tools to Ground Zero to help remove tons of steel (Fuoco, 2001). News magazines rushed out special issues featuring sobering yet heartwarming photographs of ordinary people helping each other through the carnage.[1] ABC News' Bill Blakemore (2001, para. 2) char-acterized the hastily arranged National Day of Prayer and Remembrance as "an act of national unity."

In the months following the attacks, the news media institutionalized its initially visceral and reactive coverage. *The New York Times*, for exam-ple, began a daily feature called Portraits of Grief (2001) describing the lives of people who died in the attacks on the World Trade Center.[2] Howell Raines, executive editor of *The Times*, called the feature the "pur-est example of good journalism also providing a kind of glue to a com-munity and perhaps a nation" (Raines, 2001). Magazines analyzed "the new normal," with *Newsweek's* report of "the Mets embracing the Braves at Shea Stadium" and a "'60s radical ... flying Old Glory" (Gates, 2001, p. 54) and *U. S. News & World Report's* story on a psychologist who has changed the way she treats her patients since September 11 (Simon, Howe, Reese, Huriash, & Neusner, 2001). The media also ran frequent updates on the progress of those who survived—and the families of those who didn't.

Larry King Live, for example, kept track of the pregnancy of Lisa Beamer, widow of Todd Beamer, one of the passengers on Flight 93 believed to have fought back against hijackers and forced the plane down in Pennsylvania. Biographical coverage that once would have been the softest of soft news has become an ongoing commitment of news organizations' hard-news staff.

This unprecedented and continuing coverage of the lives of ordinary people and the positive outcomes of the September 11 tragedy has caused media professionals to muse publicly on how news and journalism have changed since the "day the world changed." In the week following the at-tacks, media critic Howard Kurtz (2001) wrote,

To look at anything published before Tuesday at 8:45 a.m. ... is to realize how suddenly, dramatically, unalterably the world has changed. And that means journalism will also change, indeed is changing before our eyes. (pp. C1, C3)

Lawrence Grossman, former president of NBC News and PBS, saw "overnight" change:

> The focus of news seemed to change overnight from escapist fixation on ce-
> lebrities, stars, gossip, and the super rich to a seriousness of purpose, a con-
> cern for the truly significant news of the day, and, interestingly, a renewed
> appreciation for ordinary working people as the pillars of society—the fire-
> men, policemen, emergency workers and others who became the new, larger
> than life heroes and victims of the day. (Grossman, 2002, para. 3)

A seismic shift in journalism since September 11.

Citing Robert Lichter, president of the Center of Media and Public Affairs, columnist Fred Barnes (2001) contemplated historic changes in the press:

> For a generation now, the type of reporting practiced first in Washington and
> then nationwide has been adversarial, cynical, and highly negative. ... Since
> it was the experience of covering the civil-rights movement, Vietnam, and
> Watergate that helped create this sort of reporting, might the trauma of Sep-
> tember 11 propel the press toward a more positive, dispassionate, and ideo-
> logically impartial style ...? Robert Lichter thinks so. "There's been a seismic
> shift in journalism since September 11," he told me. "The idea of the journal-
> ist as critical outsider has been blown to smithereens." (p. 2)

Journalists were living the story, not just reporting.

How could the news not have changed? Most of those who produce national news live and work in New York or Washington and so were not just
reporting the story—they were living it. And every one had a story to tell,
like the Time, Inc., executive who described her son fleeing his office in the
World Trade Center while Time's employees braved a potentially collaps-
ing Rockefeller Center to turn out a 48-page special issue. (Kadlecek, 2001,
para. 6). The horror of "homeland" terrorist attacks forced journalists to
live the story even as they reported it. Although some reporters (such as
war correspondents) routinely carry such a burden, most news staffs were
unprepared for a tragedy that made the usual journalistic norms of objectivity and self-imposed distance seem irrelevant and even unobtainable.

As personally significant coverage becomes a new normal—fueled by atrocities such as the February 2002 murder of *Wall Street Journal* reporter Daniel Pearl in Pakistan—journalists must begin to work out the philosophical underpinnings of new journalistic norms. Veteran reporter Haynes Johnson (2001), chiding the news business's tendency toward "fragmenting of the audience," called for "a better job of reporting" and "a better job of celebrating the best in us":

> We've got to put aside our illusions and we've got to sort of unite, not just in a flag-waving moment, which is fine, but that could be a temporary moment. … We won't resolve all the hatreds, but does it mean forging new coalitions? Yes. [Does] it mean a worldwide effort in common interests? Yes, it means that. (para. 19; brackets in original)

Reporting his first visit to the former site of the World Trade Center, Johnson said that witnessing young people cheer and pass water bottles to police officers and firefighters made him feel enormously hopeful because the young people "were united with everybody else at the moment" (Johnson, para. 20).

Even before September 11, theorists about journalism were discussing—with some urgency—the news media's role in promoting unity in society. Gardner, Csikszentmihalyi, and Damon's (2001) study of the media, for example, offered the concept of *good work*—work that exhibits both excellence and ethics—as a way for journalism to assist in strengthening the human community. Now, as Gardner noted in a recent interview (Potier, 2001), "September 11 has given journalists a new lease on what they should be doing. Whether in the long run, that will re-align the domain, it's way too early to say." Journalists looking for a philosophical justification for their new or revitalized sense of being at one with their subjects may find what they're searching for in communitarianism, the "line of thought that offers the notion that the individual is interdependent with the group" (Coleman, 2000, p. 43).

Toward a Discourse of Community

Heralded by Nietzsche's cataclysmic announcement of the death of God, a pervasive grand narrative of the 20th century was *anomie*—a fundamental feeling of separation—from God, from others, from oneself. The term *culture of separation* was coined to describe the times (Bellah, Madsen, Sullivan, Swidler, & Tipton, 1985, p. 277). *Individualism* was said to undercut the public life on which the "sacredness of the human person and the inviolable order of human rights" is realized, bifurcating the self from the communities that at least partly constitute the self (Grasso, Bradley, &

Hunt, 1995, p. 3). *Collectivism*—the identity politics of viewing oneself in terms of one's membership in a certain community or social group—did not resolve the self-society split. Instead, it often amounted to tribalism, wherein one group jockeyed for its own advancement often in competition with other groups or the common good (Bidinotto, 1996).

Concurrent with the separatist turn, and perhaps as a response to it, a discourse of "community" emerged. *Connection* (or *interconnection*) frequently surfaced as a theme in feminist and environmentalist rhetorical theories, with metaphors such as "bridge" and "web" (Belenky, Clinchy, Goldberger, & Tarule, 1986). The literary, philosophical, and rhetorical worlds witnessed interest in *consensus*, "an awareness or understanding that agreements are held" (Farrell, 1999, p. 144) as a legitimating epistemological standard. Habermas (1981/1984) theorized that participants would "harmonize their individual plans of action with one another" to reach such consensus (p. 294). Even in the religious realm, *solidarity* joined the ranks of other cardinal virtues as "a key virtue needed to address the problems of our world" (Hollenbach, 1995, p. 150).

> *Communitarianism ... aims to recover the self-society union.*

The field of journalism, too, responded to fractures in the social fabric, by tapping into the discourse of community. Coleman (2000) traced journalism's response from the individualist's rights-based paradigm to the recommendations of the Hutchins Commission in 1947 and its ensuing Social Responsibility theory. The rise of investigative journalism, initiated at the turn of the 20th Century and reaching peak moments during the Vietnam War in the 1960s and the Watergate scandal in the early 1970s, intensified the journalists' sense of responsibility to the public good, understood better through Habermas' (1987) ruminations on "the public sphere." Journalists would immerse themselves in community so as to obtain first-hand (rather than third-person) perspective on reality, even sponsoring citizen input to discuss current affairs. This practice reached its height with a new journalism, in which the reporter (e.g., Tom Wolfe) was the story. The 1970s also saw the founding of the American News Service, which was devoted to news about community-building and concerned itself with the participation of "ordinary people" in democracy (Gardner et al., 2001, pp. 192–193). Throughout the 1990s, and continuing today, Civic Journalism (also called Public Journalism) sought to reinforce community solidarity (Gardner et al., p. 202). But communitarianism, the philosophy that views humans as communal beings, presents the most determined alternative to fragmentariness, individualism, and collectivism, because it aims to recover the self-society union.

The communitarian paradigm coheres around three operative principles. First, the communitarian's view of the individual is of the *embedded self*. From widely diverse perspectives, communitarians endorsed the notion that "[p]ersons are fundamentally connected, with each other and with the world they inhabit" (Frazer & Lacey, 1993, p. 102). Communitarians endorsed a social constructionist notion that "people are constituted by the social bonds within which they live" (Daly, 1994, p. 79). That social bond included the stories and myths embedded in particular communities (MacIntyre, 1994a). "Individual integrity and social decency go together," wrote Elshtain (1995), adding that society "is not a giant personification of a separate entity, 'standing over against all individuals and actively oppressing them'" (p. 101). In the communitarian paradigm, individual ontology was said to be "totally dependent on the group" or the community (Hodges, 1996, p. 136). Thus, persons were seen not merely as the central actors of their own personal narratives; they were also supporting characters in the narratives of people with whom they share community membership. Journalists who would be faithful to the notion of the embedded self were advised to view the self-society link as a key connection: "As brokers of information and ideas—honest brokers—journalists connect the personal to the public, the individual to the community" (Coleman, 2000, p. 48). In the wake of the events of September 11, 2001, journalists seem to have felt keenly the connections with people with whom they shared their common loss.

Amitai Etzioni (1993), a major architect of communitarianism, held that a "measure of caring, sharing, and being our brother's and sister's keeper" is an essential element of communitarian civic life (p. 260). Thus a second central principle of communitarianism is *reciprocity*: the notion that "each member of the community owes something to all the rest, and the community owes something to each of its members" (Etzioni, 1993, p. 263). The reciprocity endorsed in communitarianism extends beyond the person-to-person encounter and is concerned as well with relations among communities, enabling "each member community to honor its particular traditions and subculture, and to advance its interests and needs while still working with other communities to sustain a core of shared values" (Etzioni, 1996, p. 189). During the September 11 tragedy, some photographers say they dropped their cameras to help injured people while other photographers kept shooting to provide a record: Both interpreted their decisions in terms of community with people they hadn't known an instant beforehand.

A third aspect of the civic life that communitarians advocate is one fostered through *experience* or praxis, not merely doctrine or political charisma. The communitarian moral agent works to translate virtue into practice. Etzioni (1993) wrote that "moral education takes place least in classroom lectures" and that the "school should be considered *a set of expe-*

riences generating situations in which ... people learn the values of ... civility, sharing, and responsibility to the common good" (p. 259, emphasis added). Many proponents of communitarianism have stressed *shared practice* (e.g., Bellah et al., 1985; MacIntyre, 1994a, 1994b; Sandel, 1994). In company with the other two operative principles, shared experience surfaces as the highest point of human fulfillment in the communitarian perspective. Journalists covering the aftermath of September 11 were especially attuned to community acts of volunteerism to relieve mourners and public displays of gratitude for civil servants.

Community, then, is the organizing principle of communitarianism. It constitutes the theme around which the discourse of social embeddedness, reciprocal interplay, and shared experience revolve. Building upon and extending this discourse of community, Lubich lays theoretic parameters for a participatory professional journalism.

Chiara Lubich's Normative Ethic

A well-known public figure in Europe, Chiara Lubich has received numerous distinctions and awards, including 12 honorary doctorates, the UNESCO Peace Education prize, and the Council of Europe's European Prize for Human Rights. In several countries throughout the world, she has launched political and economic initiatives that favor reciprocal action. In the religious realm, she was the first Christian, the first woman, and the first lay person invited to present her experience: to a group of 800 Buddhist monks and nuns in Thailand; to 3,000 African American Muslims in the Malcolm Shabazz Mosque in Harlem, New York; and to a Jewish community in Buenos Aires, Brazil. Lubich's normative proposal for media can be described according to main purpose, typical technique, and overall moral perspective.[3] Lubich (2000) reported that many members of the Focolare Movement have been "working along these lines for years, and in different parts of the world ... in hostile or apparently impenetrable environments."

The Main Purpose of Communitarian Journalism

According to Lubich, the broad goal, or mission, of media is to promote unity. Indeed, a regular feature of the *Living City*, the Focolare Movement's monthly magazine, is Kaleidoscope: News of a world coming together. As Lubich puts it, mass media enable contact with people "to be more one, to be one" (Bangkok). The thrust of media, says Lubich, is a movement "from complexity to oneness, from fragmentation to the search for unity in real time" (CG).

At minimum, the purpose of journalism is to provide communities with a "common base of information" (Gardner et al., 2001, p. 168). Yet reporting of facts stops short of fulfilling the visionary purpose of communitarian journalism. In Lubich's view, news stories should provide more than the "5 W's"; they should also reinforce "community." As such, the journalism that Lubich envisions is a community-building agency and therefore a promoter of social change.

However, Lubich's communitarian moral philosophy is distinct from other communitarian aims espoused by Lambeth (1992) and Anderson, Dardenne, and Killenberg (1996), which stressed the mass communicator's activist responsibility in stimulating public inquiry or providing a forum for public "conversation."[4] Instead, the communitarian ethic Lubich has in mind approximates that advanced by Christians, Ferré, and Fackler (1993), which maintained that an act "is morally right when compelled by the intention to maintain the community of persons" (p. 73), and that proposed by Ettema and Glasser (1998), which promotes "solidarity—establishing an empathetic link between those who have suffered in the situation and the rest of us" (p. 189). Lubich posited a virtue ethics that recommends particular moral perspectives the communicator should bring to the communication process. Together these principles advanced by Lubich turn the media and mass communicators in service of a global objective: achieving a united world. *Unity*, then, is the cardinal virtue that Lubich proposes as the central theme of communitarian discourse and the central aim of a communitarian media ethic.

The Typical Technique of Communitarian Journalism

The second element of Lubich's normative proposal for media is *technique*. Three elements characterize the method of a communitarian journalism that would fulfill the mission of uniting. First, communication itself is essential, because, as Lubich stated, "what is not communicated is lost" (CG). Contained within this element is the notion that journalism should continue its commitment to communicating a plurality of perspectives. But plurality does not necessarily reinforce community. Instead, Lubich promotes the sharing of perspectives, which entails widening the lens of journalism to cover aspects of news to which traditional journalism has not attended.

One such neglected aspect is the positive dimension of events. A second guideline that Lubich offers, therefore, is that journalism should bring to light the congruities in human affairs. Though journalists bear a certain responsibility to report "errors, limits, and faults," Lubich (CG) pointed out, the journalist's commitment to truthfulness compels the telling of positive dimensions of reality that are also true.

A third guideline that Lubich submits as a method of achieving the noblest aspirations of media is that journalists should "make ourselves one" (CG) with those with whom they communicate. Here, Lubich affirms the value of placing the reporter on the scene. This participatory journalism replaces the emerging trends in broadcast journalism toward adding local voice-over to imported tape or film—and superimposing anchors' and reporters' figures over a virtual backdrop (Gardner et al., 2001, p. 132). Instead, Lubich advises that reporters get to know the subjects of stories as well as audiences. She also advises that reporters make themselves known: to explain their purpose or motivation. "In this way," said Lubich, "the message is not only understood intellectually, but it is also shared" (CG).

The Moral Perspective of Communitarian Journalism

The third and final element of Lubich's normative proposal for media is *moral perspective*. Lubich maintains that searching out the signs of community begins and ends with the person. "What matters is the person," said Lubich (CG). Maintaining focus on persons directs the journalist to look at self, others (the subjects of a story), and audiences/society in writing the story. Lubich sees the technologies of media as tools to be used in service of people and, in particular, in the service of uniting people. To carry out the person-centered purpose of journalism, Lubich directs journalists to make themselves one with their colleagues. Unity with colleagues creates an atmosphere that promotes greater sensitivity to aspects of community outside the newsroom. In turn, the journalist is better disposed to become one with subjects of stories and to recognize signs of community or unity "in the town square." The orientation would be one that invites a shared experience—one that solicits an experience of community and itself instantiates it. The journalist would then approach a story with a mindset that respects *the other*, searches out *the positive*, and pays attention to the congruities in current events.

Application of Lubich's Perspective in Media Professions

Lubich's moral guidelines are simple, almost prosaic. However, media professionals in the areas of print, radio, television, film, photography, and new media who have implemented Lubich's moral guidelines tell of profound effects. In a 2000 media congress convened in Castel Gandalfo, Italy, for members of the Focolare Movement who work in the media industry, participants shared their experience of consciously applying Lubich's normative ethic in their professional practice. Those experiences have been posted on a web site for media professionals to share their attempts to follow Lubich's moral proposals; three narratives are sketched later.[5]

Paul Loriga, news editor of an Italian magazine, reported his experience of his attempts to attend to the positive even in a disaster story (Netone, 2000). In reporting on an earthquake in Albania and a mudslide in Sarno, for example, Loriga indicated that he reported the adversities of those incidents but that he did not stop at those depictions. Nor was he interested in edifying or consoling readers. What guided his reporting was his realization that the story of earthquakes and mudslides consisted of more than the hardships they wrought. Like reports of ordinary heroism following the events of September 11, 2001, these stories consisted, also, of people giving themselves to help their neighbors, efforts to rebuild houses, and quiet acts of collaboration and solidarity among residents. The facts represented by these stories, then, also contained a positive dimension that Loriga felt warranted news attention. Loriga also commented on his emphasis on respecting sources of information *as persons* in his news—explaining that he looks on the interviewee not as a "new source, a lemon to squeeze, a juke-box of emotions and expressions that give color to stories." In fact, once the recorder has been turned off, Loriga said that interviewees have often confided personal or family hardships to him, a measure of unity between interviewer and news source.

Argentine radio station owners Margarita and Raul Bermudez related how they made themselves one with a listening community they sought to serve, saying that they moved away from Buenos Aires to be closer to their listeners. In their new location, the Bermudezes endured the hardships typically experienced in that community, including lack of sanitary conditions. What they saw as most lacking, however, was communication "at all levels, within institutions, between [institutions] and people, the various groups and organizations, and even between close families." Their goal became one of Lubich's first moral guideline—to promote communication within community segments: "to disseminate the activities of the community organizations; to retrieve national and cultural identity; to stimulate the local artists; … favoring the dialogue between the parts" (Netone, 2000).

A freelance television journalist in New York, Aldo Civico, described how he incorporates Lubich's teachings in his coverage of stories of crime and war. Besides attending to negative facts in stories of kidnappings and prostitution, for example, Civico has looked for small openings of hope. He described journalism as "an opportunity to know, to share the restlessness, the loneliness, the anguish of humanity" (Netone, 2000) while searching for signs of solidarity and peace.

Implications for Media Ethics

Lubich's guiding principles of communication are shown to converge in one principal ethic, unity, a normative ethic that Lubich professes is not only possible but essential to the proper function of media. Though communitarian in nature, Lubich's proposition nonetheless shifts the locus of moral discernment away from the public, the community, or—Coleman's markers—the audience and face-to-face communication. Lubich directs attention, instead, toward the communicator as both animator and surveyor of unity. The journalist both becomes one with communication participants and reports unity where it is found. Lubich's moral philosophy thus refines our understanding of communitarian mass media ethics.

The aforementioned examples of a communication that adheres to Lubich's moral proposals promote unity, not collectivism. Though the latter may be visualized as a *collage*—fragments of material incongruously pasted together (*Webster's*, 1996, p. 403)—the former has been shown to resemble a mosaic "held together by a frame and glue" (Etzioni, 1996, p. 192), a vital component of reality. This distinction is important to the journalist who would seek to capture community because it directs the communicator's attention to the congruities of human affairs. Lubich is especially interested in bonds of unity created in reciprocal action, wherein media professionals make themselves one with the other in a shared experience that "strains toward generalization … toward ideas and attitudes that embrace ever-larger segments of experience" (Selznick, 1992, p. 163).

It may be argued that applying Lubich's communitarian ethic to journalism thwarts necessary objectivity because it seems to put the journalist, charged with reporting the facts, at the service of a particular view of reality, one that stresses community or unity. And indeed, journalists adopting unity as a moral imperative do practice an empathic and participatory mode of communication, not an objectively distanced one (Ong, 1982, pp. 45–46). However, the communitarian paradigm contains its own dimension of objectivity or truthfulness, as Christians (1997) observed,

> Truth is understood as authenticity *in a social context,* and its validity is freed from the correspondence tradition. … And as we come to live inside universal *human solidarity,* we recognize that a basic list of ethical principles is entailed by it—social justice, truth-telling, nonmaleficence, and possibly others. (pp. 16–17, emphases added)

Others might object that given the terrorist attacks in 2001, the idea of a global community or human solidarity, and hence a communitarian ethic, seems utopian. However, given the media attention to unity, community, and ordinary heroes following the terrorist attacks in 2001, 9/11 may have sounded a cry for help in the way journalists practice their craft. Indeed, unity appears to have added itself to the lexicon of journalism. Lubich hopes to make that addition explicit.

Acknowledgment

I thank E. A. Macom for her editorial assistance in developing the arguments of this article.

Notes

1. *Newsweek* published an undated Extra Edition and a September 24 Special Report. *The Economist* titled its September 15–21, 2001, edition "The day the world changed." *Time* ran a special September 11 edition replete with photos of the disaster.
2. Portraits of Grief ran continuously through December 31, 2001, and periodically thereafter.
3. Chiara Lubich has addressed the subject of modern media in two major addresses: in Bangkok, Thailand, on January 5, 1997, on receiving an honorary doctorate in social communications from St. John's University; and in Castel Gandalfo, Italy, on June 3, 2000, at a Congress of Focolare members who work in the media. Direct quotations from Lubich's speeches are based on her prepared texts and are not paginated. The Bangkok address is identified in the text of this article as "Bangkok" and the Castel Gandolfo address as "CG."
4. See Craig's (1996, pp. 111–112) summary of the recent communitarian press theory of Lambeth (1992); Anderson, Dardenne, & Killenberg (1996); and Christians, Ferré, & Fackler (1993).
5. The Web site for members of the Focolare who work in the field of mass media, entitled *Netone: Media and a United World*, is http://www.netone.flars.net/The language of the Web site is Italian; translations for this article are by the author with assistance from Altavista translation software.The Web site is identified in this text as "Netone."

References

Anderson, R., Dardenne, R., & Killenberg, G. (1996). *The conversation of journalism: Communication, community, and news.* Westport, CT: Praegar.

Barnes, F. (2001, December 3). The press in time of war. *The Weekly Standard*, p. 2.

Belenky, M., Clinchy, B., Goldberger, N., & Tarule, J. (1986). *Women's ways of knowing: The development of self, voice, and mind.* New York: Basic Books.

Bellah, R., Madsen, R., Sullivan, W., Swidler, A., & Tipton, S. (1985). *Habits of the heart: Individualism and commitment in American life.* New York: Harper & Row.

Bidinotto, R. J. (1996, January). A matter of principle from liberalism to tribalism. *Liberty Haven.* (Originally published in *The Freeman, 46*, 1.) Retrieved March 1, 2002, from http://www.libertyhaven.com/politicsandcurrentevents/scandalsorpoliticalinjusti ce/matterlibtri.html

Blakemore, B. (2001, September 14). "World News Tonight," ABC News. Retrieved February 22, 2002, from http://web.lexis-nexis.com/

Christians, C. (1997). The ethics of being in a communication context. In C. Christians & M. Traber (Eds.), *Communication ethics and universal values* (pp. 3–23). Thousand Oaks, CA: Sage.

Christians, C., Ferré, J., & Fackler, P. (1993). *Good news: Social ethics and the press.* New York: Oxford University Press.

Coleman, R. (2000). The ethical context for public journalism: As an ethical foundation for public journalism, communitarian philosophy provides principles for practitioners to apply to real-world problems. *Journal of Communication Inquiry, 24*(1), 41–66.

Craig, D. A. (1996). Communitarian journalism(s): Clearing conceptual landscapes. *Journal of Mass Media Ethics, 11,* 107–118.

Daly, M. (Ed.). (1994). *Communitarianism: A new public ethics.* Belmont, CA: Wadsworth.

Elshtain, J. B. (1995). The communitarian individual. In A. Etzioni (Ed.), *New communitarian thinking: Persons, virtues, institutions, and communities* (pp. 99–109). Charlottesville: University Press of Virginia.

Ettema, J. S., & Glasser, T. L. (1998). *Custodians of conscience.* New York: Columbia University Press.

Etzioni, A. (1993). *The spirit of community.* New York: Crown.

Etzioni, A. (1996). *The new golden rule.* New York: Basic Books.

Farrell, T. (1999). Knowledge, consensus, and rhetorical theory. In J. L Lucaites, C. M. Condit, & S. Caudill (Eds.), *Contemporary rhetorical theory: A reader* (pp. 140–152). New York: Guilford.

Frazer, E., & Lacey, N. (1993). *The politics of community: A feminist critique of the liberal-communitarian debate.* Toronto, Canada: University of Toronto Press.

Fuoco, M. A. (2001, September 27). Duty calls ironworker from idyll in the forest: A volunteer confronts the pain at WTC. *Pittsburgh Post-Gazette.* Retrieved March 3, 2002, from http://www.post-gazette.com/headlines/20010927aftershocknat2p2.asp

Gardner, H., Csikszentmihalyi, M., & Damon, W. (2001). *Good work: When excellence and ethics meet.* New York: Basic Books.

Gates, D. (2001, October 8). Living a new normal. *Newsweek,* pp. 54–59.

Grasso, K., Bradley, G., & Hunt, R. (Eds.). (1995). *Catholicism, liberalism, and communitarianism: The Catholic intellectual tradition and the moral foundations of democracy.* Lanham, MD: Rowman & Littlefield.

Grossman, L. (2002, January 23). *TV in the age of globalization: Promoting mutual understanding.* [Transcript of speech to the 11th International Symposium of the Japan Media Communication Center.] Retrieved February 20, 2002, from http://www.jamco.or.jp/2002_symposium/en/paper/keynote_speech.html

Habermas, J. (1984). *The theory of communicative action, volume 1: Reason and the rationalization of society* (T. McCarthy, Trans.). Boston: Beacon. (Original work published 1981)

Habermas, J. (1987). *Philosophical discourse of modernity* (F. Lawrence, Trans.). Cambridge, MA: MIT Press.

Hodges, L. (1996). Ruminations about the communitarian debate. *Journal of Mass Media Ethics, 11*, 133–139.

Hollenbach, D. (1995). Virtue, the common good, and democracy. In A. Etzioni (Ed.), *New communitarian thinking: Persons, virtues, institutions, and communities* (pp. 143–153). Charlottesville: University Press of Virginia.

Johnson, H. (2001, October 10). Transcript of speech to the Los Angeles World Affairs Council. Retrieved February 27, 2002, from http://www.lawac.org/speech/haynes_johnson_author.htm

Kadlecek, J. (2001, November 20). Bill Moyers hosts Columbia journalism review 40th anniversary panel discussion. *Columbia News*. Retrieved February 10, 2002, from http://www.Columbia.edu/cu/news/01/11/cjr_40th.html

Kurtz, H. (2001, September 17). Journalism's surreal reality check. *The Washington Post*, pp. C1, C3.

Lambeth, E. (1992). *Committed journalism: An ethic for the profession* (2nd ed.). Bloomington: Indiana University Press.

Lubich, C. (1997, January 5). Prepared text of address upon conferral of honorary doctorate in Bangkok, Thailand.

Lubich, C. (2000, June 3). Prepared text of address to congress of the Focolare and Media in Castel Gandolfo, Italy. Excerpted in *Living City* (2000, October), pp. 16–18.

MacIntyre, A. (1994a). The concept of a tradition. In M. Daly (Ed.), *Communitarianism: A new public ethics* (pp. 121–126). Belmont, CA: Wadsworth.

MacIntyre, A. (1994b). The privatization of good: An inaugural lecture. In C. F. Delaney (Ed.), *The liberalism-communitarianism debate: Liberty and community values* (pp. 1–18). Lanham, MD: Rowman & Littlefield.

Netone: Media and a United World. (2000, June 3). Retrieved August 26, 2002 from http://www.netone.flars.net/

Ong, W. J. (1982). *Orality and literacy: The technologizing of the word*. New York: Routledge.

Portraits of grief. (2001, September 15). *The New York Times*. Retrieved February 22, 2002, from http://www.nytimes.com/national/portraits/index.html

Potier, B. (2001, November 1). The man in the mirror: GSE's Howard Gardner explores good work. [Interview with Howard Gardner.] *Harvard University Gazette*. Retrieved on February 26, 2002, from http://www.hno.harvard.edu/gazette/2001/11.01/11-gardner.html

Raines, H. (2001, December 7). Video of Raines discussing *New York Times* coverage of the September 11 attacks. Retrieved February 22, 2002, from http://www.nytimes.com/packages/html/national/portraits/20011207 raines-video.html

Sandel, M. (1994). Justice and the moral subject. In M. Daly (Ed.), *Communitarianism: A new public ethics* (pp. 79–88). Belmont, CA: Wadsworth.

Selznick, P. (1992). *The moral commonwealth: Social theory and the promise of community*. Los Angeles: University of California Press.

Simon, R., Howe, J., Reese, K., Huriash, L., & Neusner. (2001, November 12). The new normal. *U. S. News & World Report*, pp. 14–21.

Webster's new universal unabridged dictionary. (1996). New York: Barnes & Noble.

Journal of Mass Media Ethics, 17(4), 304–313

The Search for Ethical Journalism in Central America and the Failure of the New Orleans Declaration

Rick Rockwell

American University

❏ *In this analysis I use the first regional Central America ethics code to discuss the wider problems of corruption and media complicity with central governments in the region. Luis Moreno Ocampo of Transparency International has noted that to understand corruption factors one must first study formalized rules for the system. Following Moreno's suggestion, in this article I focus on the code and the actions it inspired to highlight the widespread corrupt media practices of the region. Although the code had an immediate effect, that effect has waned and in some cases has been forgotten.*

In June 1993, owners of some leading media organizations in Central America met in New Orleans in an attempt to raise standards for their news organizations and all the media of the region. The result was a 12-point document that spelled out a new ethics code for the region's journalists.

The catalyst behind the conference was a special center at Florida International University (FIU), known at the time as the Central American Journalism Program (CAJP). With the help of the U.S. government, Florida International had established the center with the aim of improving journalism throughout Central America (Heise & Green, 1996). With the Cold War over, the purpose of the center's programs was to bolster democracy in the region through the improvement of journalism. One approach toward improving journalism in the region was through improvement of ethical standards.

The leaders of CAJP set as one of their goals encouraging Central American journalists and media owners to shape their own future and set their own standards (personal communication, Charles Green, director of CJAP, February 20, 1998). Bringing key members of the Central American journalism community together in New Orleans was one major step in accomplishing that goal. The conference convened roughly halfway through the 10-year existence of the center at FIU. The impetus of the conference would prove to be a major factor in raising and bolstering standards in key instances in various countries in Central America, at least short term.

However, nearly a decade after it was drafted, the New Orleans Declaration seemed to be a forgotten document. Standards it established were implemented inconsistently, and in some cases ethics improved very little after an initial push. Even alumni of FIU's programs, expected to carry on the CAJP legacy, seemed to see the New Orleans Declaration as a product of a different era. For instance, Eduardo Enriquez, an alumnus of FIU's programs in the region and co-managing editor of Nicaragua's *La Prensa,* recently drew up a new code of ethics for his newspaper. However, Enriquez said he did not use the New Orleans Declaration as a foundation for his paper's new ethics code. He claimed he has never read the New Orleans Declaration and its code of ethical behavior (personal communication, August 8, 2001).

Theme

In this article I examine fallout, both positive and negative, of the declaration. Although the CAJP was the catalytic force behind the document, leaders of the FIU program vowed not to impose ethical standards from the United States on the region. Some of the lost legacy of the CAJP may relate to the end of funding for the program in 1998. However, in this article I attempt to delve deeper into the regional journalism culture to discover why efforts at raising standards met with little long-term success.

The inherent objective of this article is a closer look at some of the 12 standards set by these Central American media leaders. The standards themselves illuminate some of the deep-seated problems faced by journalists in the region. By using anecdotal examples, historical references, and interviews conducted in the region, I attempt to show just how large a mountain these journalists set out to climb when they gathered in New Orleans in 1993.

As a way of reflecting on the New Orleans Declaration, this article will also use various other ethical standards as a springboard for discussion. First, the code of ethics of the Society of Professional Journalists (SPJ), which bears some resemblance to the New Orleans Declaration, will be used for comparative value (Black, Steele, & Barney, 1999). Because goals of the CAJP and the New Orleans Declaration seem to have some connection to the growth of democracy in the region, this article will also reference the work of John Stuart Mill (1995). Mill's work on utilitarianism and its application to burgeoning democracies seems appropriate as Central America strives to build some semblance of democracy in the post-Cold War era.

Cracks in the Foundation

A recent example of abandonment of the principles of the New Orleans Declaration can be found in El Salvador. Enrique Altamirano, publisher of *El Diario de Hoy*, a top newspaper in San Salvador, was a member of the advisory committee of the CAJP. Using the expertise of the CAJP, Altamirano revamped his newspaper in the 1990s, importing chief editors from Costa Rica and hiring a young staff to fill the newspaper's columns (Janus, 1998). But the paper's makeover, an attempt to shift it from a past of support for rightwing death squads, appears to have been superficial.

After El Salvador's series of major earthquakes in 2001, Altamirano's newspaper became the public mouthpiece of the Salvadoran government, defending the government against criticisms of earthquake relief efforts. This recalled Altamirano's earlier relationship with the government and the ruling conservative party, ARENA. Altamirano was a vocal supporter of ARENA during El Salvador's civil war. However, with the makeover at *El Diario de Hoy*, the owner and publisher had seemed to renounce that past. The newspaper's objective facade crumbled though when the ARENA government was blasted by one of El Salvador's television networks in the wake of the quakes.

Canal 12, a television network, ran a series of stories and reports that called into question the government's response to the earthquakes. Canal 12 was the only network to carry allegations from some Salvadorans that only neighborhoods supporting the ARENA party were getting the first post-quake aid. Canal 12 also was the only media outlet in the country to cover protests by earthquake survivors about how the government handled relief efforts (Rockwell & Neubauer, 2001). *El Diario de Hoy* responded on the government's behalf by claiming that Canal 12 had staged the protests as a way of sensationalizing the news. Altamirano also penned a series of editorials attacking Canal 12's main anchorman and his program, *Hechos* (*El Diario*, January 18, January 22, 2001). Sorely lacking in any of the newspaper's pro-government attacks was proof of media fabrication.

The attacks were similar to the charges and countercharges batted between the media representing different factions during the country's civil war. Canal 12 had represented moderates and those out of favor with the conservative government during the war. The network was the first to give the country's leftwing guerrillas a media platform to speak, a fact that resurfaced in *El Diario de Hoy's* critical editorials.

Besides the newspaper's vocal attacks, the fallout from the TV network's reports was also similar to the civil war. One network reporter, Milagro Vallecillos, received a series of threatening phone calls and left the country for her own safety (Rockwell, Janus, & Neubauer, 2001).

The government, the country's leading advertiser, also substantially reduced its commercial placement with Canal 12, leaving the network in a financial crisis (Dada, Vaquerano, & Ramos, 2001). The ARENA government also engineered advertising boycotts against the network during the war (Valencia, 1994).

Consider this incident in light of the New Orleans Declaration. Altamirano, the publisher of *El Diario de Hoy*, was on the advisory committee of the organizers of the New Orleans conference and was at least a tacit supporter of the declaration. Likewise, the general manager of Canal 12 and a minority owner of the network, Jorge Zedan, was on the same advisory council.

The media flap generated by Canal 12's critical reports and the newspaper's defense of the government seems in direct conflict with the first tenet of the declaration which calls for the media to fight to maintain independence. In three subsections, the declaration spells out just how that should be handled:

1. Reject all forms of coercion of public power about freedom of expression and the search and broadcast of information and opinions.
2. Maintain the same attitude in respect to the pressure of other sectors and individuals.
3. Act on behalf of the public in the search for information and to satisfy as much as possible the right to be informed about subjects of social interest ("Declaracion de principios," 1993).

In the case of *El Diario de Hoy*, the newspaper not only ignored the government's coercion of Canal 12, but it became a de facto agent of the government, attacking the television network and the network's personnel. Without many allies, the network was left to seek help from El Salvador's special ombudsman for human rights, who is now investigating the government's actions against Canal 12 (Valladares Melgar, 2001). But through its attacks, the newspaper not only dug up old political animosities but it also undercut the spirit of free expression in the country. All three opening sections of the declaration's ethics code were seemingly ignored in this incident.

The third tenet of the New Orleans Declaration also calls for the media "to act in good faith ... to be equitable in the treatment of persons or institutions ... and always search for exactitude in information" ("Declaracion de principios," 1993). The newspaper's actions in this case seem to display tendencies which run counter to this section of the code too, especially by aiming allegations at the network that news events were staged and then providing no proof.

These two areas of the Central American code bear strong resemblance to the SPJ Code. The SPJ Code stresses the following: Seek truth and report it while maintaining editorial independence (Black, et al., 1999). It might be argued that *El Diario de Hoy* was merely providing a counterbalance to Canal 12's critical earthquake reports, much as media in Latin America and

Europe have often assumed political lines of engagement, a different editorial tradition and custom than in the United States (Waisbord, 2000). However, the truth behind the newspaper's allegations of fabrication by the television network have become a matter of a human rights investigation in El Salvador. Truth does not seem to be a major consideration in how *El Diario de Hoy* formed its reports against Canal 12. Also the newspaper's long association with the ARENA government speaks to the lack of independence in its decision-making surrounding this incident. By any measure, the newspaper would seem to have failed to uphold both the U.S. code and the Central American ethics standard.

Canal 12's actions in reporting citizen complaints about the ARENA government and its handling of disaster relief are certainly undertaken in the spirit of utilitarianism promoted by Mill. Conversely, the role of *El Diario de Hoy* in providing pressure against Canal 12 seems to be an example of anti-utilitarian behavior. In this instance, the newspaper acts in concert with a government attempting to silence one of its critics. Mill (1995) wrote derisively of such acts: "All silencing of discussion is an assumption of infallibility .... He who knows only his side of a case knows little of that" (pp. 73, 76). This philosophy would seem to condemn the actions of a media system that tries to quash discussion or use coercive means to stifle discussion. Mills' view also seems to support the fourth section of the Central American ethics code which in part reads, "Our mission in the search for the truth is to make it possible that in the media there are expressions of different viewpoints and to see counter positions" ("Declaracion de principios," 1993). This is another area of the code abandoned by *El Diario de Hoy* and its publisher.

A Different History

Nearly 10 years have passed since the New Orleans Declaration, but the impact of the new Central American code has seemingly slowed to a halt over those years. Yet, the immediate climate for ethics that the code generated held out hope for the future.

Less than 2 weeks before the New Orleans Declaration was signed, journalists in Guatemala had instigated the ouster of President Jorge Serrano (Alamilla, Perez, & Taylor, 1996). Serrano had tried to suspend the constitution and seize dictatorial powers, a so-called "self-coup" modeled after Alberto Fujimori's power grab in Peru. Media protests against Serrano's new censorship orders drew protests which, sparked by the media, proved to be the president's undoing and he fled for the safety of exile in Panama. The Guatemalan example seemed to show that the media did have power when they upheld ethical standards such as refusing to buckle to coercion, and supporting the rights of all media outlets to give voice to their various points of view.

This event proved to be one of the spiritual underpinnings of the declaration. The essence of the Guatemalan struggle is contained in part of the declaration's first tenet: "Reject all forms of coercion of public power about the freedom of expression and the search and broadcast of information and opinions" ("Declaracion de principios," 1993).

But the media in Central America were just beginning to demonstrate their newly found strength of purpose. Following the signing of the New Orleans Declaration, news managers in Honduras took steps to end corruption in their newsrooms. At *El Tiempo* in San Pedro Sula, editor Vilma Gloria Rosales, cited the new ethical codes as her main reason for striking out against open payoffs to her reporters.

In a way, Rosales' intervention was forced upon her by the mistake of a corrupt reporter. The organizer of the reporters at *El Tiempo* who accepted regular payments from Honduras' National Election Tribunal let these clandestine activities slip out into the open. He mistakenly left a list of participants and the amounts they were due on the photocopier at *El Tiempo*, where they were discovered by management. In the spirit of the newly adopted ethical code, Rosales not only confronted the reporters in her newsroom, but she published their names, and shared the list with her competition. Despite being threatened at gunpoint by the reporter who had originally forgotten the bribery list, Rosales followed through in cleaning up the problem (personal communication with Maria Antonia Martinez, managing editor of *La Prensa*, March 23, 1998).

At Rosales' crosstown rival, *La Prensa*, managing editor Nelson Fernandez also printed the list. Fernandez and Rosales both fired members of their staffs who had accepted the payments from the government. Because *La Prensa* and *El Tiempo* are among the most respected and popular publications in Honduras, this very public action was influential in driving overt corruption out of most newsrooms in Honduras (personal communication with Maria Antonia Martinez, managing editor of *La Prensa*, March 23, 1998). Both papers used their influence to also encourage the drafting of firm policies to prevent corrupt practices at most of the media organizations in the country.

In 1995, the spirit of the New Orleans Declaration would reach Panama. The newly formed investigative unit at *La Prensa* of Panama City chose corruption in the media as its first major investigation. Bravely, the newspaper revealed which prominent reporters were taking bribes from the National Assembly, and the list included one of their own political reporters. *El Panama America, Critica Libre*, and *El Siglo* all followed with extensive coverage of the media scandal (Guerrero, 1995).

These actions seem in line with the essence of the New Orleans Declaration. The declaration's first point calls on journalists to retain independence and declares "autonomy is requisite and indispensable" ("Declaracion de principios," 1993). This echoes the call for independence that is one of the cornerstones of the SPJ Code.

The bold actions in Panama and Honduras to strike back at corrupt reporters also are tied to the declaration's second point which in part reads, "Journalists and administrators of the media must not benefit personally, more than what is legitimately implied in their managerial functions or professional functions" ("Declaracion de principios," 1993).

The Central American code also deals directly with the economic pressures on journalists in the region. The sixth point of the code echoes earlier sentiments by warning, "Conflicts of interest must be avoided at all costs" ("Declaracion de principios," 1993). However, this point further spells out that ethical behavior of media owners includes paying workers a living wage and providing basic work conditions that promote ethical behavior.

"A media owner who knows that his journalist is making $300 or $400 a month and who sees him drive into the media parking lot in a BMW he either gave it to him or is participating in the corruption," noted Sandra Maribel Sanchez, a reporter at Honduras' Radio America who has reported on official corruption in her country and faced death threats for her reporting (Fliess, 1999).

After the reporting scandals in Honduras in 1993, newsroom managers at some newspapers were successful in limited ways in raising wage levels for reporters. However, 5 years later, at Honduras' *La Prensa*, the managing editor of the paper, Maria Antonia Martinez, was sanguine about the return of corruption to her newsroom. "It never really left," she said, "it just went under the table. They know we will penalize them if they are caught so they are secretive (personal communication, March 23, 1998). In 1998, Martinez, who had disciplined one of her reporters caught accepting illicit payments, seemed to accept that unless salaries were raised significantly, corruption would remain just below the surface.

In Panama, some newspapers like Panama City's *La Prensa* reacted to the corruption scandals by raising salaries and bringing in trainers from the CAJP and other journalism organizations to promote ethics. Although the average reporter's salary in Panama was about $300 per month during the 1990s, a *La Prensa* a profit-sharing program changed that economic picture for employees. Some doubled or tripled their annual wages with payments from the profit-sharing plan (personal communication with Charles Green, director of CAJP, February 20, 1998).

Attempts at stopping corruption through exposure and wage hikes aligns with the final point of the Central American code: "Financial independence is the instrument for a robust journalistic independence. For this, the media must not obtain privileges or favoritism from public powers or private powers" ("Declaracion de principios," 1993).

Retrenchment

Somewhere in the last decade, the propulsion behind these important changes lost speed; the fuel ran low. Somehow the New Orleans Declaration no longer seemed to connect with the realities of day-to-day journalism in the region.

In Honduras, Carlos Flores, the owner of *La Tribuna*, campaigned successfully to become the country's president in 1997. A key campaign aide noted that without the newspaper as a base of operations for Flores' political aspirations, he might never have been elected (personal communication with Rodolfo Dumas Castillo, March 24, 1998). Flores' successful candidacy was an important development in Honduras. He was the first from a successful group of families that had developed not only into an entrepreneurial oligarchy during the 20th century, but also into an oligarchy that controlled almost every major media outlet in the country.

The president soon began using his connections within the media to control the message about his administration. Not only did President Flores remain influential at his own newspaper, but journalists accused the president of calling media owners to manipulate coverage. Journalists accused the president of having stories spiked and of using his influence to have his journalistic critics fired or demoted. Meanwhile, those who supported his political positions were promoted or given jobs in his administration (Chasan, 1999). Flores' tactics seemed to once again legitimize influence peddling and cronyism in the zone of exchange between politics and journalism in Honduras.

In Guatemala, in the years since the signing of the New Orleans Declaration, Mexican media owner Angel Gonzalez acquired all of the nation's television networks along with a significant chunk of the nation's radio spectrum. In the presidential elections of 1999, Gonzalez supported Alfonso Portillo, a candidate of the extreme right.

During the campaign, Jose Zarco, a popular journalist, emerged as a major critic of Portillo. Zarco rented time for his independently produced television program on one of Gonzalez's channels. After Portillo's successful campaign and inauguration, Zarco's program was canceled and Gonzalez would not agree to make any other time available for Zarco's news magazine. Some media outlets accused the new president of colluding with Gonzalez to rid the system of a critical journalist ("Nuevo golpe," 2000). In return, Gonzalez's brother-in-law, Luis Rabbe became Portillo's Minister of Communications. This was convenient for Gonzalez, who circumvents foreign-ownership laws for the media by keeping his properties in the name of his wife, a Guatemalan citizen (Vanden Heuvel & Dennis, 1995). Rabbe would eventually leave office after a corruption scandal and criticism that he had hired a mob to attack the newspaper *elPeriodico*, another vocal critic of the Portillo administration (Bounds, Emmott, & Webb-Vidal, 2001).

Conclusion

What these incidents seem to describe is a top-down, hierarchical journalism in Central America. Clearly, the atmosphere has changed in countries like El Salvador, Honduras, and Guatemala, when the owners of major media outlets return again to the traditional roles of media organizations that become economic and political weapons in a nation's political system. This is power some pledged to abandon in favor of a higher calling of media public service. That public service was at the core of the New Orleans Declaration.

Stepping back from the anecdotal developments for journalism on the troubled isthmus of Central America, it is possible to discern the push and pull of new trends, and the move toward higher standards in some corners of the profession. However, observing the process is like watching a still patch of ocean. Certainly there are undercurrents, waves, schools of fish darting about; plenty of motion. But the end result still appears to be a flat patch of sea when observed on the macro level. At that level, media owners have returned to old habits by supporting conservative politicians and oligarchies in the region. Media barons are still working to limit voices critical of the governments and conservative entrepreneurs who are the region's real powers. The examples cited here of the critics they have tried to stifle are just a few from the region in the past few years. There may be currents shifting this system, like the New Orleans Declaration and the CAJP, giving the appearance that greater freedoms and higher standards will be forthcoming. But in the end, real advancement is hard to detect.

Because of the hierarchical nature of the media in the region, until media owners truly embrace a standard like the New Orleans Declaration, Central America will continue to languish in the poor habits of the past. Some of the solution also means the communication system must be opened to smaller, alternative media voices, instead of allowing the domination of a few powerful owners, like Gonzalez in Guatemala, or even President Flores in Honduras. Current conditions encourage a system where powerful media owners undercut ethical standards to keep advertising flowing from its main source: the central government. This type of collusion also stifles voices that would criticize the system, as with Canal 12 in El Salvador. Only when the system allows space for critical voices will the still patch of ocean break up into the stormy sea of divergent opinions that truly makes up a free media in a democratic system.

References

Alamilla, I., Perez, J., & Taylor, R. (1996). *The Guatemalan media: The challenge of democracy.* Guatemala City: Cerigua.

Black, J., Steele, B., & Barney, R. (1999). *Doing ethics in journalism* (3rd ed.). Needham, MA: Allyn & Bacon.

Bounds, A., Emmott, R., & Webb-Vidal, A. (2001, July 4). Press finds it a struggle to stay free in Latin America. *The Financial Times* (London), p. 3.

Chasan, A. (Ed.). (1999). *Attacks on the press in 1998.* New York: Committee to Protect Journalists.

Dada, C., Vaquerano, R., & Ramos, C. (2001, April 28). Esta en crisis Canal 12 [Channel 12 in crisis], *La Prensa Grafica* (San Salvador), p. 13.

Declaracion de principios del periodismo Centroamericano [Declaration of principles of Central American journalism]. (1993, June 12). *Pulso.* Reprinted in III *Congreso Latioamericano de Periodismo* [Third Congress Program of the Center for Latin American Journalism].

El Diario de Hoy (San Salvador). (2001, January 18). Cocinando "Reportajes" [Cooking Reports], p. 14.

El Diario de Hoy (San Salvador). (2001, January 22). En respuesta a Don Mauricio [In Response to Don Mauricio].

Fliess, M. (1999, September 13). "Honduran press called tarnished by corruption," *free!* [The Internet Journal of the Freedom Forum]. Retrieved November 16, 1999, from http://www.freedomforum.org/international/1999/9/13mediaatmill.asp

Guerrero, A. (1995, April–July). Las relaciones peligrosas [Dangerous relations]. *Pulso*, pp. 16–17.

Heise, J. A., & Green, C. H. (1996). An unusual approach in the United States to Latin American journalism education. In R. R. Cole (Ed.), *Communication in Latin America: Journalism, mass media and society* (pp. 51–76). Wilmington, DE: Scholarly Resources.

Janus, N. (1998). *Latin American journalism project: El Salvador.* Washington, DC: USAID.

Mill, J. S. (1995). On liberty, as excerpted. In S. R. Knowlton & P. R. Parsons (Eds.), *The journalist's moral compass* (pp. 71–81). Westport, CT: Praeger.

Nuevo golpe la libertad de prensa [New coup against press freedom]. (2000, February 4). *Prensa Libre*, p. 12.

Rockwell, R., Janus, N., & Neubauer, K. (2001, May 24). Expose could signal end of El Salvador TV news magazine. *Pacific News Service.*

Rockwell, R., & Neubauer, K. (2001, July 29). Media feel government pressure. *The Sun* (Baltimore), pp. 1C, 6C.

Valencia, F. (1994). El poder economico y los medios de comunicacion [Economic power and the communication media]. In J. Ordinez (Ed.), *Periodismo, derechos humanos y control de poder politico en centroamerica* [Journalism, human rights and the control of political power in Central America] (pp. 89–95). San Jose, Costa Rica: InterAmerican Institute of Human Rights.

Valladares Melgar, M. A., special ombudsman for the defense of human rights in El Salvador. (2001, January 22). [Letter from San Salvador to Carlos Rosales, Press Secretary for Salvadoran Pres. Francisco Flores].

Vanden Heuvel, J., & Dennis, E. E. (1995). *Changing patterns: Latin America's vital media.* New York: The Freedom Forum Media Studies Center.

Waisbord, S. (2000). *Watchdog journalism in South America: News, accountability, and democracy.* New York: Columbia University Press.

Journal of Mass Media Ethics, 17(4), 314–317

Either Ignorance or Freedom

Kevin Klose
National Public Radio

❏ *Following are excerpts from the keynote speech delivered to the second of the Collo-quium 2000 series on applied media ethics by Kevin Klose, president and chief execu-tive officer of National Public Radio. Mr. Klose spoke in the Robert E. Lee chapel at Washington and Lee University in Lexington, Virginia, November 2, 2001. This col-loquium sought to unearth global values in media ethics.*

Broadcasting and journalism, if they are done right, can help with the dilemma Jefferson posed to the Republic at around the time of the writing of the Declaration of Independence. He said that a people cannot be both ignorant and free.

Broadcasting in its slightly more than a hundred-year history has been a hexed medium, both extremely powerful in societies ready to use that power in ways that would find common ground, but also becoming ex-tremely powerful in societies headed for destabilization, debasement, and ultimately immorality. In the 20th century the largest genocide in history was preceded by a single dictatorial voice, a hectic, insane, nonstop voice that took captive radio in what had been a civilized European nation with some historical sense of order and common cause as a driving engine of what became the Holocaust. This pattern has repeated itself over and over throughout the history of broadcasting. The genocides in central Africa in the 1990s and the ethnic wars that swept through Yugoslavia in the 1990s were preceded by the takeover of what had been essentially independent and disparate broadcasting and media by one set of voices who fomented issues of xenophobia, of fear, of separation that caused people to look at their neighbors in completely different ways. The paradigm of what their reality was started to shift. Once it shifted to where it could not come back, the only way to make up differences was to shed blood.

So, broadcast is a very complicated medium and as the 21st century be-gins to unfold, we know that the electronic media, broadcast media or multicast media, are not going to go away.

Important in this is the uniqueness of what has been created in the United States of America in the way of public broadcasting. Not to specifi-cally dwell on National Public Radio, but it is a standard by which some kinds of public broadcasting could be measured. What's unique about National Public Radio and the public radio system in the United States of America is that it has no real state support, except in a very minimal way. It is essentially a voluntary relationship between listeners who support their local stations and, in the case of National Public Radio, a national program provider. Most of the 300 voting members in the National Public Radio Community create most of their programming themselves. Only roughly 22% to 25% of their programming on any one day is provided by National Public Radio. So the power of the local station resembles the power of the community to reflect its own values, to deal with its own issues, and to be relevant to its community within the reach of its transmitters. In that regard, there is almost no other system in the world in broadcasting that resembles this one. It dispels ignorance essentially supported by voluntary contributions of listeners.

*A voluntary relationship
between radio and listeners.*

At National Public Radio 45% out of budget of about $100 million a year comes from member stations, and they derive 80% of their revenue typically from their listeners. The core relationship is a voluntary relationship between the listener and the programming providers. About one third of our income comes from corporate underwriting. And we get about one fourth of our income from charitable foundations and nonprofits and some individuals. One percent of the program monies of our budget come from federal funds for which we compete with other broadcasters. For example, the National Science Foundation supports science reporting, and the National Endowment for the Humanities helps us do some of our cultural programming. Those are very powerful relationships. They define a unique reality in public broadcasting and if we could spread the philosophy, it would be very helpful in other places. It resembles in a particular way consensual self-government and the mechanisms of self-government and citizen participation in government, which are the core of the governance experience in the United States that have been so since before the Revolution. Self-government and self-empowerment run hand-in-hand. If a public broadcaster is heavily supported by some state entity, the danger of being influenced by that entity is very high. The possibility of having multiple sets of voices and perspectives and ideas presented on that state medium are going to be very, very much reduced.

How do you adjust and project whatever the values and the ethical standards are in society and make them comprehensible or acceptable? I think that you come back to the very beginning, winding up where Jefferson began, as I quoted him earlier: "A people cannot be both ignorant and free."

The media in any country have to be measured by that straightforward gauge. Entertainment is one thing, but information and the empowerment of individuals to make informed decisions through information is the way to judge the ethical standing of broadcast organizations globally.

Now, does it come down to accuracy? Yes, whose accuracy? Whose fact? Whose truths? That's where it gets much harder, but the dedication is to bring information, and that is how to get to a very, very clear standard.

The Internet has made the world very different, immediately accessible to itself and to others in a way that surpasses broadcasting. Again we don't know all that will happen on the Internet, but the fact that somebody can go on in their home computer sitting 11 time zones from here, and call up on that local computer a Web site that has Washington and Lee University or has National Public Radio on it or has the BBC or *The New York Times* or any of the other hundreds and hundreds and hundreds of media outlets that are now on the Web, tells you something about the transparency, not just of the American media reality, but of the transparency of the world in this whole new medium. The Web, as we know, is without boundaries and without time limits. Information available on the Web in pictures, in video, in audio and in text has none of the confinements of broadcasting. It can be universal and personal and unique, and because it is interactive, offers the power to interact with those media in a whole different way from broadcasting. When it becomes interactive, it changes the nature of the dynamic in a fundamental way. We don't know where it's all going to go but it has an enormous impact in the fact that it is there for us already and supports and is augmenting the reality of the broadcasting media. It is there for millions of people who otherwise would never hear National Public Radio programming or never see CNN. Those realities are part and parcel of what we all are facing.

---

*... enhancement of the act
of being a citizen.*

In my estimation, the moment for the kind of nonprofit, noncommercial programming that can be done in the public media is unique and very powerful and can reach people in very, very special ways. The values you see in public media include the presentation of ideas and programming without regard to selling something and without regard to rating points and market share. Public media can do that to enhance the act of being a citizen in a society and to offer information, analysis, and cultural presentations to people in a setting very different from a commercial setting. It is really not driven by entertainment. It is driven by information and regard for the audiences and the viewers.

The power to reach worldwide through other broadcast systems and the Internet we take very seriously at NPR in Washington. We believe that the responsibilities that have come our way by the changes that have gone on in the commercial media in this country have given us the responsibility to think very carefully about foreign audiences as well, even though we do it only in vernacular American English. We don't do it in any other language. The reality is the power of the American civil society with all of the ups and downs, and all of the criticisms and shortcomings, the power of the American civil society with all its diversity and its expanding diversity has made us to other people very interesting. Globally, people want to know about the power of American civil society, not just because American generals have nuclear weapons but because our civil society has been so powerful in envoking people's hopes to create new lives for themselves and to run their democracy as they see fit. This is part of what comes out of NPR. We are not a mass medium engaged in entertainment but a medium engaged in information and access to ideas and cultural presentations. What's interesting to me is that foreign interest in what we produce and what we provide to our member stations remains extraordinarily powerful, and it is rising.

Global broadcasting can be a part of that if the people who lead it and commit to it and support it commit to it themselves.

Journal of Mass Media Ethics, *17*(4), 318–327
Copyright © 2002, Lawrence Erlbaum Associates, Inc.

Cases and Commentaries

The *Journal of Mass Media Ethics* publishes case studies in which scholars and media professionals outline how they would address a particular ethical problem. Some cases are hypothetical, but most are from actual newsroom experiences, corporations, and other agencies. We invite readers to call our attention to current cases and issues. (There is a special need for good cases in advertising and public relations.) We also seek names of both professionals and academicians who might write commentaries. I wrote the following case. It raises a fundamental question about the ethics of editorial judgment that is truly universal and global: What kinds of information about and images of their world do people need from media of mass communication? That question, more than any other, frames media ethics.

It thus seems especially fitting for this special issue of the journal.

Editor: Louis W. Hodges
Knight Professor of Ethics in Journalism
Washington and Lee University
Lexington, VA 24450

The *Phoenix* and Daniel Pearl

Editors at the *Boston Phoenix,* an alternative newspaper, chose to publish photographs of the murder of *Wall Street Journal* reporter Daniel Pearl. The pictures contained a shot of Pearl's severed head being held up for display by one of his killers. Online the paper linked to sections of a videotape apparently showing Pearl's actual beheading.

The journalism community immediately reacted—mostly in disdain—to the June 6, 2002, publication. Gary Hill, KSTP-TV Minneapolis and chair of the Society of Professional Journalists' Ethics Committee, wrote, "While it [the photo of the severed head] may represent a sort of grisly 'truth' it will do nothing to advance our understanding of terrorism, kidnapping, or murder. It seems to directly contradict one of the direct lines in our [SPJ's] code, 'Show good taste. Avoid pandering to lurid curiosity.'"

Fred Brown, recently retired from *The Denver Post* and co-chair of SPJ's Ethics Committee, wrote, "It's just lurid, adolescent voyeurism. Do people really need to see pictures of severed heads to know that the authorities aren't lying to them? I think only the most paranoid conspiracy theorists require that kind of affirmation, and for everyone else who's curious, it's just grisly pandering."

Some scholars are concerned that, through well-intentioned efforts to sanitize the world they depict, journalists may distort their audiences' picture of the world—thereby giving an inaccurate and dangerously false impression that the world is not as grisly and threatening as it really is. Given that concern, it would seem reasonable that the *Phoenix* made a morally defensible choice to publish.

Stephen M. Mindich, publisher of the *Phoenix*, wrote of the Pearl murder and pictures, "This is the single most gruesome, horrible, despicable, and horrifying thing I've ever seen. The outrage I feel as an American and a Jew is almost indescribable. If there is anything that should galvanize every non-Jew hater in the world—of whatever faith, or of no faith—against the perpetrators and supporters of those who committed this unspeakable murder, it should be the viewing [of] this video."

Others have expressed concern over other issues, including questions of taste, effects on young children, causing further pain for Pearl's family, whether the newspaper's motives were merely self-serving, effects on the public's perception of journalists and journalism (credibility), the newspaper's First Amendment RIGHT to publish, the need for warnings about graphic footage, and the ethics of NOT giving people the choice to view the tape.

Commentary 1
There's a Third Way

People of good will could come down on either side of publishing the photograph.

My contrarian position is that the journalist's job isn't to supply either pure Pablum or pure horror. The significance of publishing the photograph is not primarily a matter of freedom of the press, ethics, or taste. Rather, to use the wording of the 1947 Hutchins Commission, I think the media should provide "A truthful, comprehensive, and intelligent account of the day's events in a context which gives them meaning."

In other words, the fuss about publication of the photo in an alternative newspaper is a tempest in a teapot—except for those who knew Pearl, and those who murdered him.

Emotional reactions to this publication probably have little to do with traditional ethics. It's not new. We've thought about the taste and propriety of photos and video of sudden death many times before—people jumping from the upper floors of the World Trade Center, the maltreatment of American corpses shown in *Black Hawk Down*, the *Challenger* explosion, or the dead body of a U.S. serviceman washing up on a beach early in World War II. Automobile crashes and other violent consequences are often illustrated in broadcast and print media.

Each instance led to complaints based on taste, dignity, privacy, and "news value." Reasonable people often disagreed: Closeups of military casualties might result in lowered morale, make recruiting more difficult, and reduce public approval of the combat—as the U.S. military (and the peace movement) found out during the Vietnam conflict.

One may argue that depiction of violent death—page 1, prime time, or the Saturday cartoons—may have negative effects on children, but I believe children need to learn that death is a part of life to grow into adulthood. We learn to deal with such pictures family by family, person by person, and year by year. (There are, however, legitimate moralistic objections to making the videotape of Pearl's murder and mutilation easy—through Internet linkage—for the voyeuristic and immature to obtain.)

Whether the *Phoenix* should have published the photo was a decision for the *Phoenix*. While the *Phoenix*'s actions were "the buzz," it is very unlikely it would pick up long-term readership or advertising revenue from its sensational coverage of Pearl's murder. The *Phoenix* might have wished to tell Jews in Greater Boston "we're on your side" in the hope that support would follow.

Titillation for its own sake is indefensible. If one is going to show a horrible picture, one needs a valid purpose. If the only reason for the newspaper's coverage was to appeal to our baser instincts, it deserves to lose both readership and advertising. I think it more likely that the politically active publisher of the *Phoenix* was trying to show that the side he didn't support had acted like barbarians. This is within the American journalistic tradition, provided the bias is acknowledged. It is also possible that, under competitive deadline pressure, it just seemed like a good idea to publish the most sensational photo, regardless. I doubt if the *Phoenix*'s editorial staff considered the Utilitarian value of the decision, or even the Kantian categorical imperative that the public is entitled to know or see everything. (Personally, I wouldn't have run the photo because it makes me uncomfortable and I see no overriding social value in it.)

It is too bad the brouhaha over pictures of Pearl's murder overshadows other important journalistic questions. Where is the context of the story? (That is, was Watergate *solely* a third-rate burglary?) Why was Pearl enticed and murdered, and why did his killers want the publicity? Was he murdered in such a fashion because he was an American? A Jew? Or a journalist?

I mourn with the Pearl family and realize how the unexpectedness and inhumanity of his death added to their grief. After agonizing over the uncertainty caused by his kidnapping, Pearl's family had to face the fact that he had been brutally murdered. But, unless they wanted to, they didn't have to view either the videotape or the still photograph. The Boston *Phoenix* is unlikely to be one of the newspapers in the Pearl home. Television and cable channels have given warning before airing such material. It wasn't presented in "ambush" fashion.

To whom is it helpful to emphasize the brutality of Daniel Pearl's murder? Nobody. I don't advocate minimizing Pearl's death, but figurative gasoline on a fire is both personally dangerous and likely socially harmful. For example, after seeing Pearl's head held high, reporters and photographers may show more caution than is warranted, further reducing the already limited coverage we have of foreign affairs, particularly in the Middle East, and political leaders may make decisions and take risks that are shortsighted and potentially disastrous. Of course, this may have been the murder's purpose.

The "public's right to know" is not absolute—and I'm not speaking here of the limitations that the current administration in Washington would like to place on the press. Professionally, I believe this right should be modified by the responsibility of the professional news media to select, reflect, focus, edit, and explain significant events. If shock and horror are used by the media, the goal for their utilization should be to promote understanding rather than revenge, to provide context rather than immediate gratification from the pornography of violence, and to make the world a less hostile environment. After all, publishing such a grisly photo isn't justifiable in the eyes of most of the reading public; and it shouldn't be in ours.

By Mike Kittross, Editor
Media Ethics
Boston

Commentary 2
When Does It Become Unethical
to Withhold Truths From Readers?

Seek truth and report it. Minimize harm. The tension between those core principles from the Society of Professional Journalists' Code of Ethics is at the heart of the debate over whether the *Phoenix* acted ethically when it published a photo of Daniel Pearl's severed head and offered readers a link to the gory video of *The Wall Street Journal* reporter's brutal murder.

First, an admission: I minimized harm to myself by choosing not to look at the *Phoenix* picture or follow its link to the video. Count me among those who were shocked and shed tears when I learned that Pearl was mocked as a Jew and brutally slaughtered with the camera running. I sympathize with readers who complained that it was hurtful for the newspaper to confront them, without warning, with such a grisly scene.

Family or friends of Mr. Pearl could be especially traumatized by turning the page and seeing his severed head. Pearl's grieving family is surely not comforted knowing that people can watch in morbid fascination as he is murdered and mutilated. These are real harms journalists should minimize while seeking truth.

When the SPJ Ethics Committee debated online whether those harms overrode the informational value of the images, I was among a small minority who saw any value in having readers see the actual murder. Fred Brown, the committee's former chairman, dismissed the *Phoenix* visuals as adding little to truths that were already apparent.

But was the newspaper gratuitously indulging lurid tastes, or did the images reveal important truths about the character of Pearl's executioners, who looked into his face; listened to his words; knew him to be a son, husband, and expectant father; then brutally ended his life and celebrated his death by mutilating his body?

Readers already knew radical Islamists were willing to crash jetliners into skyscrapers and kill thousands of innocent people whose faces they would never see. The Pearl video showed they were willing to look into an innocent man's eyes and butcher him—a scene that should reveal truths to Islamic moderates who sometimes defend the "just cause" of these desperate men and offer them financial and political support.

The job of journalists has always been to hold up the mirror so people can see themselves and their world as they really are. In my reporting classes, I tell students to write stories that show rather than tell. Can we brand it unethical when photojournalists show the events that reporters try so hard to describe in words? I cannot forget John Hersey's book depicting what happened at the first Ground Zero, Hiroshima. Was Hersey acting unethically in telling the painful truth about what atomic bombs can do to human flesh, how eyeballs melt into sunken sockets and sheets of skin peel from scorched but living bodies? Those truths have value today as nuclear powers Pakistan and India teeter on the brink of war. Graphic images of the holocaust rebut the lies of revisionists, and photos of lynchings in the south remind Americans of our own brutal and racist history. Would the most recent genocide in Rwanda have continued as long as it did had photos shown neighbors hacking each other to pieces with machetes?

As is often the case, the Pearl photo and the video both inflicted pain and revealed truths. Had I been in the shoes of the *Phoenix* editor, I would have reached a split decision—link to the video with an appropriate warning, but do not publish the still photograph. We ought to minimize harm to readers who choose not to see graphic violence by warning them in advance and giving them the opportunity to opt out. Instead, the editor flung the photo of Pearl's severed head into the faces of readers, who may have included people who knew him since he once worked in the area. In contrast, the video link allowed readers to make their own choices, whether they were seeking those unpleasant truths or, like me, avoiding the pain of watching a man die. Our new interactive world has forever altered the journalist's role as gatekeeper and arbiter of taste and allowed us to let readers make more of their own choices.

That doesn't mean journalists should pander to morbid curiosities by routinely posting gory photos of accidents and victims on Web sites. Violence as entertainment is reprehensible, particularly when real victims and families can be harmed. Before we expose readers or viewers to graphic visuals, we should think long and hard about whether they are newsworthy and necessary, whether their value as truth outweighs harm we inflict on families and victims. Even when they offer important truths, photos as graphic as the Pearl visuals should be offered only after readers are warned. While I chose not to view the Pearl video, I am uncomfortable deciding that others should not be allowed a choice to see images that offer important truths about how a brave journalist tried to write about one side in the most important news story of our time—the war against terrorism—and instead became its victim.

Comments in letters written by *Phoenix* readers and posted at the paper's Web site suggest that readers want choices and are capable of making them thoughtfully.

One reader suggested the real pandering was by media who declined to let readers see the photos based on fear of public outrage and rebuke, disguising their censorship as a decision based on journalistic responsibility and righteousness.

By Ted Frederickson
Professor of Journalism
The University of Kansas

Commentary 3
Where the *Phoenix* Went Wrong

The *Boston Phoenix* maintains its decision to create and promote a Web link to the Daniel Pearl murder video was "clear cut" (Editorial, June 6–13, 2002). In fact, the *Phoenix* failed to adequately meet five essential criteria, proposed here as a framework for decision making in similar cases.

1. It failed to demonstrate thoroughly that the propaganda is newsworthy so that drawing attention to it is not mere sensationalism. Though the

Phoenix failed to meet this test, it would not have been difficult to comply. Despite Pearl's death months earlier, the tape itself was news because it used images of his murder to inspire more of the same via its worldwide dissemination. Publisher Stephen Mindich advanced the newsworthiness argument only by implication, however (Publisher's note, June 4, 2002), and he was accused of sensationalizing an old story.

2. It failed to demonstrate thoroughly that making the propaganda available is sound journalism, not pandering to perverse curiosity. Such a case can be made regarding the Pearl tape. One of the journalist's most compelling duties is to give citizens a chance to understand the news as fully as possible. ("Seek truth and report it thoroughly," to quote the SPJ Code of Ethics.) Access to the tape allows those who so choose to add another dimension to their understanding of the case. Columnist Richard Cohen, for instance, argued that written accounts, still photos, or the sanitized excerpts presented on CBS news did not sufficiently convey to him the essence of the tape. Only by experiencing the sounds (the mixed tone of terror and hope in Pearl's voice as he recites scripted propaganda) and only by seeing the images of murder was he able to see Pearl as a person, not an abstraction. Only by watching the tape was he able to confront directly the palpable evil of the perpetrators (*Washington Post*, June 20, 2002).

Unfortunately, in a publisher's note and later editorial justifying the link, Mindich and his editors did not justify the journalistic soundness of their decision. Only in press interviews did Mindich spell out a rationale similar to Cohen's, but by then it sounded like rationalization because he was under attack as a heartless sensationalist.

3. It failed to acknowledge in detail the harms that might stem from making the propaganda more widely accessible. In creating the link, promoting it, and generating wide controversy about it, Mindich presumably increased the video's audience and drew many people to it who were not typical *Phoenix* readers. This addition to the audience might well have included children who could be disturbed by its content, "skin heads" and terrorist sympathizers ogling for inspiration, and sadistic voyeurs for whom Pearl's murder was only entertainment.

The paper did acknowledge in passing that terrorists and anti-Semites might draw inspiration from the tape (Editorial, June 6–13, 2002). But the *Phoenix* did not thoroughly itemize harms or discuss them in depth as an ethical problem. That left the paper vulnerable to charges of recklessness.

4. It did not demonstrate that providing access to the propaganda fulfills a journalistic purpose while minimizing harm so that the benefits outweigh the costs. Mindich did say his aim was to galvanize viewers of the "despicable and horrifying" tape against the perpetrators (Editor's note, June 4). And the *Phoenix* acted to limit some harm through warnings that the material was graphic, disturbing, and not suitable for children. But,

contradictorily, the paper also printed a still photo of Pearl's severed head that was readily accessible to children. Moreover, those clicking from *Phoenix* to Prohosters.com, the video site, would have found a hot link to Ogrish.com, which specializes in graphic color photos of gory rape–murder victims, mutilated testicles, and the like. The *Phoenix* thus made it easy to click to a world where victims are mere objects and the suffering of others a source of perverse pleasure.

The *Phoenix* might have minimized harm effectively had it rejected the idea of linking to unfiltered propaganda and instead imbedded the murder video in a much longer mixed media editorial of its own. The idea is to fasten an ethical frame to the murder tape tightly enough to deter anti-Semites, terrorist sympathizers, voyeurs, and children from viewing it. That would leave an audience mainly of thoughtful adults seeking to deepen their understanding of anti-American hatred and violence. And it would allow a sound cost–benefits justification for providing access to the murder tape.

Such a presentation might begin with a segment on Daniel Pearl as a three-dimensional human being. It would explain why the case is still newsworthy (see earlier text). Moral philosophers and theologians, including Muslims, would weigh in, some pointing out that it is hard to imagine a grosser breach of Kant's admonition against treating a human being merely as a means. Not only did the perpetrators slaughter an innocent noncombatant because of what he symbolized, they further objectified him as a visual aid for more violence.

Guests like Richard Cohen would then explain how, for them, there was no substitute for watching. Only at this point would the 3-min murder tape appear, preceded by a warning of graphic content, and followed by a somber sign-off.

The package would be designed so viewers could not fast-forward, fast-reverse, or fast-click to the murder footage. That would fend off children, because most would find the opening 25 min boring. It would drive away anti-Semites, incipient terrorists, and voyeurs, many of whom would balk at sitting through interminable minutes of ideologically disagreeable or disappointingly wholesome material. It might even make the tape less painful to the victim's loved ones by affirming Pearl's humanity and using the video's horrifying power against its makers—a kind of ethical jujitsu.

5. The final criterion: *Do not proceed unless you are satisfied your proposed action implies a universal rule for similar cases.* What sort of rule could we draw from the actions of the *Phoenix*? Condemn propaganda that incites murder but always promote access to it, even for those who might be incited. It is hard to imagine a world where responsible news organizations would advocate that. On the other hand, one could draw a Kantian imperative from the alternative approach suggested earlier: news outfits should encourage viewing of violent propaganda if and only if they imbed the ma-

terial in a presentation that promotes ethical insights while deterring violence and sensation seeking.

By Christopher Hanson
Assistant Professor of Journalism
University of Maryland

Commentary 4
The Decision-Making Method Is Basic

Let's focus solely on the methodology available to reach an ethical decision. The *Phoenix's* legal right to publish the photos and to link to the video is not in dispute. What officials at the paper and Web host assert to be a legal right would not be disputed by most ethicists. It is the morality of publishing the photos that is cause for debate and analysis.

The love of, or fascination with, a good photo or image, not its journalistic value, can often be the driving force in publishing photographs. Employment of good ethical decision making by news staff can readily challenge the urge to use photos and images for the sake of prurient appeal. This type of constructive discussion can generally be started by asking the questions "What is the journalistic purpose of the photograph?" and "What are my ethical concerns?"

In this case, officials with the *Phoenix* said their moral duty is to bring the harsh reality of a violent terrorist group to the attention of the American people and to show readers firsthand the horrifying effects of terrorism. Those who oppose publishing the photos may find the *Phoenix's* photos to be nothing more than "shock images" intended to scare more than enlighten readers. Or, they may argue the paper took dramatic steps to reinforce a reputation that separates it from the mainstream press. In such an argument, opponents may contend the paper has, in effect, chosen to become a newsmaker instead of news provider through controversial decisions. To this end, a valuable question would be "what are the competing values that come into play in this situation?"

Likewise, a discussion of the photos should most likely involve asking questions of necessity. For example, is it necessary to show the images of a severed head to convey the message of terrorism? Would it be sufficient in making an editorial point of the horror of terrorism to say that terrorists decapitated Pearl? Do the photographs provide additional information that helps readers understand the events surrounding Pearl's death? Do they enhance the value of the editorial and its viewpoint? Do they detract from the point being made?

Further discussion needs to include the harmful effects it may have on the stakeholders of these published photos and video. Obvious stakeholders would include Pearl's family and friends and readers of the paper or viewers at the Web site. What moral obligation does the paper have to the family? The readers? If the *Phoenix* staff believes that it has a moral duty to inform people of the atrocities of war, is it greater than the duty to spare readers and the Pearl family emotional harm?

Placement of apologies on the Web site suggests that officials felt some sense of moral obligation. But apologies were offset by a statement of their First Amendment rights to use the images. Nevertheless, they seemed to have an ethical concern over the photos' harmful effects on family members and friends of the murdered journalist. What responsibility does the editor or publisher have to ensure that readers understand the reasons for publishing such photos? Can the paper defend its actions?

In this case, Mindich goes to great lengths to defend the paper's decision. His explanation in his paper, on the Web site, and in journalistic trade publications and mainstream media suggests a concerted effort to explain his paper's rationale.

Those deciding whether to publish the photos might also have considered ethics codes. Many newspapers acknowledge the use of codes whether from a national organization, such as the Society of Professional Journalists (SPJ) or the National Press Photographers' Association (NPPA), or a code from the paper's staff.

Such a code would seem helpful in making a decision on the use of the photos. The SPJ Code of Ethics makes four points relating to the use of graphic images. Under the title "Minimizing Harm," the code says journalists should, show compassion for those affected adversely by news coverage; be sensitive when seeking or using interviews or photographs of people affected by tragedy or grief; use good taste; and avoid pandering to lurid curiosity.

The NPPA code states that "no report can be complete if it is not possible to enhance and clarify the meaning of words. We believe that pictures ... are an indispensable means of keeping people accurately informed." It concludes, "Common sense and good judgment are required in applying ethical principles."

In nearly every case, the value of such ethical discussion is elevated by standard inclusion of several staff members—including reporters, photographers, and editors—in the methodology.

Finally, future ethical decisions should incorporate the public's views. Careful pulse monitoring on these issues can help establish a sense of moral duty for the paper.

By Kevin Smith
Managing Editor
Times-West Virginian **(Fairmont, WV)**

Journal of Mass Media Ethics, 17(4), 328–336

Book Reviews

As always, the book review editor seeks energetic, thoughtful reviewers for books, software packages, films, and other media ethics materials. You may contact the editor, as listed here, to suggest an essay topic, a book, or a reviewer.

Editor: Deni Elliott
Practical Ethics Center
The University of Montana
Missoula, MT 59812
elliottd@mso.umt.edu

The Good Life Through Good Works
A Review by Albert Borgmann

Gardner, H., Csikszentmihalyi, M., & Damon, W. (2001). *Good work: When excellence and ethics meet.* New York: Basic Books. 300 pp., $26.00 (Hbk).

At a time when for most people the meaning of work lies in paying the rent and when in ethics we aim no higher than at blamelessness, a book titled *Good Work: When Ethics and Excellence Meet* is most welcome. The book, moreover, is written by three social scientists who have made their mark by moving in their different ways beyond the empirical and descriptive confinements of their disciplines.

Excellence in this case is first-rate work in one's domain, and ethics is a devotion to honesty and the common good. The core of the book are reports on the state of excellence and ethics in genetics and journalism, based on substantial interviews of over a hundred geneticists and the same number of journalists. The results are not surprising on the whole, but they have the great benefit of sharpening and supporting our intuitions.

Geneticists find themselves well-aligned with the appreciation and support of society whereas journalists are distressed, and often despairing, at the intrusions of commercialism and the lack of careful and thoughtful readers and viewers. But, as the authors never tire of telling us, geneticists must avoid complacency, and journalists may make the most of their crisis. More important, good work and devotion to high standards is still found in journalism, although teachers of journalism will be dismayed to see the authors report,

> The good-work methods examined thus far are solutions that journalists have worked out either on their own or with peers or mentors. We did not find a single instance of a strategy learned from a school of journalism, a training program, or a book or manual. It appears that the field has virtually no systematic way of imparting the methods that journalists actually use—or, if there are such ways, they are not particularly memorable or effective. (p. 205)

This passage touches on the bleakest issue that is implicitly conveyed by *Good Work*. Lay people as well as scholars like to imagine that, if only the issues closest to their hearts would get an airing in the media, the health and excellence of the body politic would begin to improve. But journalists cannot even investigate a public discussion of what ails and pains them most. We are inclined to blame the heavy hand of corporate control for this. Our darkest suspicion tells us, however, that we, the people, may have sold our civic birthright for ever more consumption.

Before I turn to criticisms of *Good Work*, I must stress the significance and soundness of the book. It is a landmark in discussing moral excellence rigorously and trenchantly. It is unwavering in its respect for the nonnegotiable dignity of truth. It is vigorous and compassionate in its concern for social justice. And it has an engaging and illuminating story to tell.

The material that surrounds the two core chapters is, however, of uneven quality. In the preface and the introductory chapter, the authors seem to be so taken with the significance of their task and each other's importance that the tenor of this part verges on sanctimony. Similarly, the penultimate chapter on "Restoring Good Work in Journalism and Genetics" strikes me as bland and strenuously well-intentioned, whereas the last chapter brings out the observations and criticisms that I had been waiting for throughout the book.

Although *Good Work* shows commendable awareness of social injustice, it would have cleared the air and protected the book from unfair criticism, had the authors pointed out the obvious—that for most working people in this country, for the janitors, waiters, retail clerks, fast food workers, assembly line workers, and on and on, good work in the sense of the book is not so much imperiled as it is simply unavailable. It is largely and so far inevitably bad work by the standards of expertise, creativity, and responsibility.

As for professional people, good work is a *three*-sided affair. Such work must be not only first-rate and ethically responsible; it must also be conducive to the good life. It is a recurring theme in the three chapters on genetics (though less so in the chapters on journalism) that work, expertly done and done in the public interest, can nevertheless deprive its practitioners of family life, leisure, and balance and eat away at their very substance (pp. 64–66, 67, 99–100, 105, 106–107, 183). It is strange that the best and the brightest among us have typically failed so to arrange their affairs that work is an element, rather than the enemy, of the good life.

Although the good life of the elite is crippled by hyperactive work, the good life for the rest of us is eroded by mindless consumption. We should not be surprised that business and industry are glad to oblige us, and their expansion is manifest in our lives, to put it with increasing censure, as privatization, commercialization, and commodification. But the root cause and responsibility rests with us, the consumers. This sad state of affairs is well described in the book's concluding chapter. A more explicit and thorough-going awareness of commodification and consumption, however, would have given the overall argument more coherence and vigor.

But let me conclude with the crucial point. *Good Work* takes up a terribly neglected issue, and in doing so it practices what it preaches—work that is expertly done and shows a fine sense of civic responsibility.

❏ *Albert Borgmann is Regents Professor of Philosophy at the University of Montana, Missoula.*

Scoop Hungry or Market Driven
A Review by Chris Roush

Kurtz, H. (2000). *The fortune tellers: Inside Wall Street's game of money, media and manipulation.* New York: Free Press. 331 pp., $26.00 (Hbk).

Striving to be the first to break major news stories such as multi-billion dollar acquisitions, print and broadcast business journalists now operate in a "high-energy environment" in which "normal news standards melt" in a bid to "scoop each other on the latest wisp of a possibility" (p. 305), according to Howard Kurtz in his book exploring the relationship between the financial media and Wall Street.

Although *The Fortune Tellers* isn't meant to be an examination of the ethics of business journalists, Kurtz does an excellent job of raising many questions about how financial news is reported. "In business, unlike politics, the reporting of rumors is deemed fair game," writes Kurtz. "Journalists ... are used every day by CEOs, by Wall Street analysts, by brokerage firms, by fund managers" (p. xiv).

As a business journalist for more than a decade, I admit that I've seen many of the practices documented by Kurtz. The issue, however, is that much of what Kurtz details in this book has become accepted practice in business journalism today in an attempt to disseminate information about companies and their stock prices to as many people as possible.

Reporting and writing about the rumors and prognostications of Wall Street experts, I would argue, is the most ethical thing a business journalist can do. Why shouldn't the part time investors who watch CNBC or are readers of the *Montgomery Advertiser* in Alabama have access to the same information, even if it is often rumor and speculation, being spread through brokerage houses by professional investors?

The opinion of these people is a valuable commodity, and any utterance by a professional investor is voraciously dissected by others. That's no different than a City Hall reporter quoting a consultant from the same political party about the mayor's budget for next year. Is expert commentary less credible if it's commentary from someone with a vested interest? In virtually every case I've seen, business journalists have bent over backwards to disclose that these analysts and managers hold positions in the stocks in which they are discussing.

In addition, I can't remember all of the times the chief executive officer of a publicly traded company told me something specifically designed to boost the stock price of his company—or to hurt the stock price of a competitor. But if the Home Depot CEO says his company is going to open 200 stores next year instead of the 150 it originally planned, shouldn't that comment be reported so that everyone has a chance to analyze it? Savvy business journalists would immediately take such a statement and call investors and analysts who follow the company to gauge whether the news is going to be viewed positively or negatively by Wall Street. That's not rarely questioning the motives; that's analyzing the news.

The job of a business journalist has become that of making sure every investor no matter how big or small has access to whatever news—and rumors—are out there moving stock prices. The business journalist is not telling investors to buy or sell that stock by reporting the rumor. They are giving the reader or watcher every piece of information affecting a company's stock price. Isn't that what they're supposed to do?

To be sure, Kurtz is dead-on in criticizing business journalists who write about companies in which they own stock. But such investing has been condemned or severely curtailed in every newsroom in which I've ever worked. And business journalists should be calling into question, as Kurtz argues, the motives of analysts touting stocks simply so their firms can gain investment banking business from those companies. I see that happening more and more every day on CNBC, in the *Wall Street Journal,* and in other publications.

However, business journalists are, for the most part, concerned daily about the ethical implications of how their reporting moves stock prices. And Kurtz has plenty of examples to back that up. He notes that CNBC and The Street.com regularly discuss relationships between investment banking firms and the companies being touted by the firm's analysts. He points out that CNBC often criticizes stock pundits for making bad predictions on the direction of the overall market. And he details how *Wall Street Journal* reporter Steve Lipin regularly inserts caveats into stories about pending mergers and acquisitions.

Kurtz' own extensive documentation shows that business journalists aren't the ethical ignoramuses that his blanket statements imply.

❏ *Chris Roush is an adjunct professor in the Journalism Department at the University of Richmond.*

Fish in Water: Life in the Mediated World
A Review by Diane Rubinow

Gitlin, T. (2001). *Media unlimited: How the torrent of images and sounds overwhelms our lives.* New York: Metropolitan Books. 288 pp., $25.00 (Hbk).

Years ago my roommate moved out and took the communal television. I haven't had a TV in my home since. Over time my electronic deficiency has provoked so much discussion that I seldom mention it anymore. Though the questions directed toward me are fairly uniform, such as what do I do while eating (eat) and do I miss it (no), judgments about my TV-less state vary. But frowns, raised eyebrows, or outright mentions of my oddness are increasingly giving way to comments about this lack as being "good" or indicative of self-control. Now not having a TV has a new label and meaning. According to sociologist Todd Gitlin's *Media Unlimited: How the Torrent of Images and Sounds Overwhelms Our Lives,* I am a secessionist, someone who takes "direct, personal action" by seeking shelter from the media storm. This is just one of the coping strategies that Gitlin says we humans have developed to navigate the media saturation that is characteristic of modern American culture.

By discussing secessionists, however, I am beginning in the middle. The intellectual launch point for Gitlin is actually a new way of perceiving the media. Like fish that don't seem to be cognizant of their watery surroundings, we often overlook the fact that the mass media "has become our familiar world." The next step in this line of reasoning might have been a mention of why this particular interpretation is worthy of attention. Although the author didn't provide this information until page 120, I'll save you the suspense.

In the face of avoidable violence, disease, inequality, oppression, poisoning, and other global afflictions, it makes sense to worry about the public cost of media bounty, to fear that it distracts from civic obligations, induces complacency and anesthesia, and works to the advantage of the oligarchs.

Because measures of media saturation are available from other sources, factoids describing the enormity of the deluge are minimal. Instead the deliberation centers on the historical origin of media's move from accessory to a central component of our civilization. In presenting this look back, what emerges is (surprise!) the idea that the media torrent exists because we want it. Mythology may fault supply side corporations and marketers. But falling production costs and the use of media as sales mechanisms are only half the story. Demand also drives saturation. Sifting through theorists to find support for his ideas, Gitlin lights on Georg Simmel (German sociologist 1858–1918). Drawing heavily on Simmel's work, the fusing of the two thought processes looks like this: As sentient beings, people are ruled primarily by emotions and the need to feel connected to others. But in the money economy, people must organize their lives around a paycheck. Feelings, therefore, need to be squeezed into the interstices of our moneymaking roles. The devaluation of feelings plus the interactions with legions of strangers inherent in modern life result in a population that is always leery, constant users of a game face. We have become blasé and cynical. Mass media comes to the rescue by providing an outlet through which we can access "disposable feelings" that are available on demand. Further, the "crowding together of heterogeneous impressions" also allow us to alleviate the tedium that is a by-product of the division of labor.

Another characteristic of media as experienced at the dawn of the 21st century is the bat-out-of-hell pace. It is the feeling of hurriedness as well as the saturation that contributes to the overall sensation of being in the midst of a torrent. "Look back fifty years, and it is hard to resist the impression that the movies were slower, newspaper and magazine articles longer, sentences longer and more complex, advertising text drawn out" (p. 88). We want speed in the media because it provides safe thrills. We also want speed in our lives—up to a point. Though instant access to everything makes life easy, the prospect of spontaneous combustion as we edge toward the speed of light looms.

But no matter that we are partially responsible for the media's saturation and speed. The torrent that is somewhat organic and somewhat imposed has become grotesque. What to do? No individual can absorb all that is being proffered. This is where the idea of being a secessionist comes in. This category is one of the strategies that help modern folks deal with the media onslaught. To cope with the intensity we transform ourselves into fans, critics, paranoids, exhibitionists, ironists, jammers, secessionists, and abolitionists. These titles are meant to be a tool set to introduce the media concept rather than hard and fast archetypes, and it is also suggested that we may each form a personal pastiche that changes over time. At the core of any stratagem is the same principle. Each assists people out of, away from, around, or into an offshoot of the torrent. Unfortunately, because we have spent so much time and energy alternately bathing in and dodging and weaving the deluge, societal obligations have fallen by the wayside. Politics and civic participation, most unfortunately, are both way-down-on-the-list afterthoughts. The importance of this implication and the negative impact on our nation and world cannot be overstated.

By picking up *Media Unlimited* you are entering into an unstated contract with the author. You are agreeing to not just read but also to think about what is being said and perhaps to re-evaluate your own ideas as well. Simple-minded opinions that are oft repeated but sans merit are defrocked. Further, Gitlin's fresh take on subjects that you *thought* you understood is valuable, particularly to students of the media. The poetic quality of the writing style is sometimes a pleasure to read and makes even straightforward ideas polished and interesting. Unfortunately, part of the forced thought process is due to a structure that is occasionally convoluted, making some concepts more difficult to absorb than is necessary. Ideas are also repeated in and across chapters. The range of topics is admirable, but the value and the relation of some to the overall subject is unclear. Because of these irregularities, on balance this book is for media scholars only. For others, an article would have sufficed.

❏ *Diane Rubinow recently completed an interdisciplinary MA in media and ecology at New York University.*

Mainstream Media: Liberal Agendas Abound
A Review by Dana Rosengard

Goldberg, B. (2001). *Bias: A CBS insider exposes how the media distort the news.* Washington, DC: Regnery Publishing. 240 pp., $27.95 (Hbk).

Bernard Goldberg's *Bias: A CBS Insider Exposes How the Media Distort the News* came out late last year to quite a bit of fanfare. Reviews appeared in *The New York Times* ("A Network Veteran Bites the Hands That Fed Him," December 13, 2001) and *The Washington Post* ("Goldberg on CBS: Nothing Good to Report," December 3, 2001) and the Emmy Award-winning author made a stop on the ratings leading network morning television show. With nearly 30 years at CBS News, Goldberg had something to get off his chest about his business and his bosses. In *Bias*, he recounts how he tried and tried to make his point inside the halls of CBS News until he could wait no longer, going public with his views in a 1996 editorial in *The Wall Street Journal* writing, "that too often, Dan (Rather) and Peter (Jennings) and Tom (Brokaw) and a lot of their foot soldiers don't deliver the news straight, that they have a liberal bias, and that no matter how often the network stars deny it, it is true" (p. 12).

The allegation of liberal bias in the media is not a new one, but with *Bias*, Goldberg put the claim out there in best-selling fashion. And he paid the ultimate price for his published whistle blowing. Goldberg is no longer an employee of CBS News.

Once rated by *TV Guide* as one of the 10 most interesting people on television, Goldberg explains his claim early in this book describing bias as not "so much political bias of the Democratic-versus Republican sort," which he says clearly exists, but rather "the problem comes in the big social and cultural issues, where we often sound more like flacks for liberal causes than objective journalists" (p. 22), he writes. And he blames the bias problem on the media elites of journalism who he sees as being hopelessly out of touch with everyday Americans.

Goldberg gives professional journalists and students of journalism alike plenty of industry fat to chew on. Where is the broadcast news agenda set? (By *The New York Times* and *The Washington Post* claims Goldberg.) How race sensitive should we be? (So much so, as Goldberg claims, that accurate video is dropped to prevent possible offense?) Should tough questions be voluntarily dropped to get an interview?

And ethical dilemmas abound in *Bias*. For instance, Goldberg writes about a CBS producer-reporter in the Miami bureau covering a story about two white men who were accused of abducting a black man, forcing him at gunpoint to drive to a remote field and setting him on fire. A senior producer in New York City told the reporter to change *Black* to *African American*, the term considered more progressive in some circles.

What would you do if you were the reporter in Miami?

The reporter told the New York superior that the black man wasn't African at all, but Jamaican.

What would you do if you were the producer in New York?

What happened, as the story is told in Goldberg's book, is that the senior producer in New York said, "Change it to African-American or the story doesn't get on the air."

The change was made. The factual error was broadcast.

In *Bias*, Goldberg makes Dan Rather out to be a Mafia-like bully: hypocritical, deceitful, and mean. Yet he defends himself against charges that he's feuding with the CBS anchor and claims he wrote this book not to take on Rather but to address a nagging problem that none of the big shots would take seriously. It was about the liberal biases, he writes, that overwhelm straight news reporting.

Regardless of where you place yourself on the political continuum, *Bias* is a good read: interesting as it is disturbing.

❏ *Dana Rosengard is an assistant professor in the Department of Journalism at the University of Memphis.*

Books Received

Borjesson, K. (Ed.). (2002). *Into the buzzsaw: Leading journalists expose the myth of a free press.* Amherst, NY: Prometheus. 275 pp., $26.00 (Hbk).

Knightley, P. (2002). *The first casualty: The war correspondent as hero and myth-maker from the Crimea to Kosovo.* Baltimore: The Johns Hopkins University Press. 592 pp., $19.95 (Pbk).

May, W. F. (2002). *Beleaguered rulers: The public obligation of the professional.* Louisville, KY: Westminster John Knox. 286 pp., $24.95 (Hbk).

Norris, P. (2002). *Digital divide: Civic engagement, information poverty and the Internet worldwide.* New York: Cambridge University Press. 320 pp., $20.00 (Pbk). $60.00 (Hbk).

O'Neil, R. M. (2002). *The First Amendment and civil liability.* Bloomington: Indiana University Press. 185 pp., $37.95 (Hbk).

SUBSCRIPTION ORDER FORM

Please ❏ enter ❏ renew my subscription to:

JOURNAL OF MASS MEDIA ETHICS

EXPLORING QUESTIONS OF MEDIA MORALITY

Volume 18, 2003, Quarterly — ISSN 0890–0523/Online ISSN 1532–7728

SUBSCRIPTION PRICES PER VOLUME:

Category:	Access Type:	Price: US/All Other Countries
❏ Individual	Online & Print	$40.00/$70.00

Subscriptions are entered on a calendar-year basis only and must be paid in advance in U.S. currency—check, credit card, or money order. Prices for subscriptions include postage and handling. Journal prices expire 12/31/03. **NOTE:** Institutions must pay institutional rates. Individual subscription orders are welcome if prepaid by credit card or personal check. **Please note:** A $20.00 penalty will be charged against customers providing checks that must be returned for payment. This assessment will be made only in instances when problems in collecting funds are directly attributable to customer error.

❏ **Check Enclosed** (U.S. Currency Only)   **Total Amount Enclosed $_____**

❏ **Charge My**: ❏ VISA   ❏ MasterCard   ❏ AMEX   ❏ Discover

Card Number _____   Exp. Date____/____

Signature_____
(Credit card orders cannot be processed without your signature.)
PRINT CLEARLY for proper delivery. STREET ADDRESS/SUITE/ROOM # REQUIRED FOR DELIVERY.

Name_____

Address_____

City/State/Zip+4_____

Daytime Phone#_____E-mail address_____
Prices are subject to change without notice.

For information about online subscriptions, visit our website at *www.erlbaum.com*

Mail orders to: **Lawrence Erlbaum Associates, Inc.,** Journal Subscription Department
10 Industrial Avenue, Mahwah, NJ 07430; (201) 258–2200; FAX (201) 760–3735; journals@erlbaum.com

LIBRARY RECOMMENDATION FORM

Detach and forward to your librarian.

❏ I have reviewed the description of the *Journal of Mass Media Ethics* and would like to recommend it for acquisition.

JOURNAL OF MASS MEDIA ETHICS

EXPLORING QUESTIONS OF MEDIA MORALITY

Volume 18, 2003, Quarterly — ISSN 0890–0523/Online ISSN 1532–7728

Category:	Access Type:	Price: US/All Other Countries
❏ Institutional	Online & Print	$345.00/$375.00
❏ Institutional	Online Only	$290.00/$290.00
❏ Institutional	Print Only	$290.00/$320.00

Name_____Title_____

Institution/Department_____

Address_____

E-mail Address_____
Librarians, please send your orders directly to LEA or contact from your subscription agent.

Lawrence Erlbaum Associates, Inc., Journal Subscription Department
10 Industrial Avenue, Mahwah, NJ 07430; (201) 258–2200; FAX (201) 760–3735; journals@erlbaum.com